DOWN EAST

A Maritime History of Maine

DOWN EAST

A Maritime History of Maine

LINCOLN P. PAINE

TILBURY HOUSE, GARDINER, MAINE
OPSAIL MAINE 2000

Tilbury House, Publishers
2 Mechanic Street
Gardiner, ME 04345
800-582-1899

OpSail Maine 2000
P. O. Box 451
Portland, ME 01401
207–541-7421

First edition July 2000.

10 9 8 7 6 5 4 3 2 1

Cataloging-in-Publication Data
Paine, Lincoln P.
    Down East : a maritime history of Maine / Lincoln P. Paine.
        p. cm.
    Includes bibliographical references and index.
    ISBN 0-88448-222-7
    1. Maine--History, Naval. 2. Shipbuilding--Maine--History.
    3. Navigation--Maine--History. 4. Shipping--Maine--History. I. Title.

F19 .P35 2000
387.5'09741--dc21   00-055954

Frontispiece: *Dark Harbor Fishermen* (1943) by N. C. Wyeth. Courtesy
Portland Museum of Art.

Designed on Crummett Mountain by Edith Allard, Somerville, Maine.
Layout by Nina DeGraff, Basil Hill Graphics, Somerville, Maine.
Editing and production by Jennifer Elliott and Barbara Diamond.
Printing and binding by J. S. McCarthy Printers, Augusta, Maine.

FOR

Victoria Kaiulani and Madeleine DuGuay

and all the other young Mainiacs

Contents

ONE   *A Sense of Place*   3

Physical geography has played a decisive role in the history of Maine and its people. This chapter describes the state's geography, the ecology of the Gulf of Maine and its rich marine life, and how these natural conditions have shaped life in Maine.

TWO   *The European Discovery of Maine*   12

European interest in North America was a natural extension of the voyages of exploration by Christopher Columbus and his contemporaries. While some dreamed of gold and spices, it was fishermen and trappers who pioneered the settlement of coastal Maine.

THREE   *The Coming of the English*   21

Formal settlement of Maine was first tried in 1607, the same year as Virginia's Jamestown Colony. Although the Popham Colony was abandoned after one winter, English fishermen were well established on the islands by the time the Pilgrims reached Plymouth in 1620.

FOUR   *"For the good and securitie of England"*   28

Apart from fish, colonial Maine's most important export was wood, especially trees that could be used for warship masts. As the English settled the interior, their relations with the Abnaki and the Abnakis' French allies led to frequent warfare. At the same time, merchants engaged in trade to England and the West Indies began to resent interference from and taxation by the Crown.

FIVE   *Revolution*   43

Despite its distance from the major theaters of conflict, Maine played a significant role in the American Revolution. Machias was the site of the first naval engagement of the war, and Castine of the country's worst naval defeat. Portland was burned, Benedict Arnold ascended the Kennebec en route to Quebec, and John Paul Jones's first overseas command was built at Kittery.

SIX   *Independence and Dependence*   50

Maine ports and merchants prospered in the first two decades following the Revolution. Their dependence on international trade made them especially vulnerable to the effects of President Jefferson's ill-conceived Embargo in 1807, and again during the War of 1812.

Foreword

IMAGES OF MAINE. An evergreen-topped rockbound coast. Surf crashing and foaming in the kelp. Fog, often. Wood smoke carried across a reach or a bay, from a camp or perhaps a shipboard cookstove. The great tidal rivers, Saco, Kennebec, Penobscot, and St. John, perforate almost the entire state, and provide not only fresh water for the brew that is the Gulf of Maine but also highways to transport the bounty of the interior ultimately to ports around the world. The bones of a once-proud ship moldering in a cove. Pot buoys and lobster boats and lobster men and women. Yachts and canoes and kayaks. Oil tankers. A lighthouse clinging to an ocean ledge. Independence. Remoteness. Sturdiness. Tradition.

Maine, of perhaps all the fifty states, has only a thin veneer over much of its past—maritime and otherwise. Maine today has been obviously shaped by and is still under the very strong influence of its geography, its topography, and its hydrology.

In this very fine book, Lincoln Paine has laid down the framework for an understanding of the maritime history of Maine in a most enjoyable fashion. He successfully relates the population and the landscape of today to their historic foundations. He does so with liberal doses of interesting and evocative first-person anecdotes. This is a book that can be read in an evening and yet should certainly find a place in one's reference library. Rather than supplant the efforts of prior historians, it helps put their work into context. One will, we feel, refer to this work again and again.

This book, in its clarity and lack of pretension, was due to be written. The occasion that sparked its creation was the visit in the summer of the year 2000 to Portland of a fleet of traditional sailing vessels under the auspices of OpSail Maine 2000. As organizers of this event, our board saw that this grand spectacle of tall ships could be given greater significance if it served not as an end in itself, but as the cornerstone of a broad-gauge education program. To that end, we inaugurated the Maine Maritime Heritage Trail, to create a network among the scores of maritime heritage sites and organizations around the state, and published this book, which puts the efforts of these institutions in historical and geographical context.

People are attracted to Maine for elemental reasons. In great measure the attraction is based on the maritime and riverine nature of this place. For those of us fortunate enough to live here, the images of maritime Maine are everyday facts of life. For others, those whose circumstances dictate that Maine be sampled firsthand only every now and again, the images need to be conjured up and savored from time to time. For all of us with an affinity for this magnificent state, and for its rich and mesmerizing maritime tradition, this book will assist in making relevant one aspect or another of that heritage and in providing the context for a still-recognizable modern feature of that history. Lincoln Paine has provided us a very useful navigational aid for which we should be thankful.

RAdm. Richard I. Rybacki, USCG (Ret.) Thomas R. Wilcox, Jr.
President Executive Director
OpSail Maine 2000 Maine Maritime Museum
Portland, Maine Bath, Maine
June 2000

Preface

DOWN EAST: *A Maritime History of Maine* was commissioned as part of the educational program for OpSail Maine 2000, the first international gathering of tall ships in Maine since the end of the era of working sail in the early 1900s. As such, it is intended to complement the broader educational mission of this event, which is to highlight the surviving evidence of Maine's maritime heritage, whether in the form of museum and library collections, historic ships, or merchants' houses spared the wrecker's ball.

Down East offers an overview of the state's centuries-old maritime history. It is intended as an introduction to this fascinating subject, and an invitation to explore it further either through reading or by setting out on the Maine Maritime Heritage Trail to visit some of the scores of historic sites around the state in which the state's river, lake, and seafaring heritage is reflected. While a few institutions and artifacts are mentioned in the text, this is a narrative history, not a reference catalogue of things or a timeline of events.

This book is not the first to tackle the intricacies of maritime Maine in all its diversity, and I have been fortunate in having at my disposal William Hutchinson Rowe's *A Maritime History of Maine* (1948) and Roger Duncan's more recent *Coastal Maine: A Maritime History* (1992). In addition to these comprehensive histories, I have drawn on the work of scores of authors and historians who have examined in greater depth particular aspects of maritime Maine and what role the state's specific maritime activities have played in local, domestic, and international affairs.

In preparing this book, I have been fortunate to rely on the advice and counsel of the Maine Maritime Museum's executive director Tom Wilcox and its library director Nathan Lipfert, maritime historian Nick Dean, and author and fish broker John Snyder. The manuscript has benefited enormously from their critique and observation. Such errors as survived their scrutiny (or were introduced after their review) are mine alone. I would also like to acknowledge my colleagues at OpSail Maine 2000, especially Richard Rybacki, president; Bill Brennan, director of waterfront operations (and former commandant of midshipmen of the Maine Maritime Academy); Don Yeskoo; Merle Hallett; and Laura Limoge.

For their help with the art program: Herb Adams; John Byrne; Rosemary Mosher, for her excellent maps; Genetta McLean, Bates College Museum of Art; Jan Fisk and Carol Dienstmann, Brick Store Museum; Pamela Belanger and Angela Waldron, Farnsworth Art Museum; Stephanie Philbrick, Maine Historical Society; Maine State Library; George Carhart, Osher Map Library, University of Southern Maine; Michelle Pecoraro, Peabody-Essex Museum, Salem, Massachusetts; Maggie Beals, Portland Harbor Museum; Kristen Levesque and Sarah Chase, Portland Museum of Art; Kristen Crean, Tate House; and the University of Maine Museum of Art, Orono.

I also received help of one sort of another from Hal Fessenden, Arthur Layton, John Rousmaniere, Laura Fecych Sprague, Phineas Sprague, Bud Warren, Jan Zenter of the Maine Maritime Academy, Triss Critchfield and Pam Wright of Waynflete School, and the subscribers to the Marine History Information Exchange Group (e-mail: MARHST-L@POST.QUEEN-SCU.CA), hosted by Queens University, Toronto.

Jennifer Elliott of Tilbury House moved mountains to undertake publication of this book within the limits of a compressed timetable, and has been as fully engaged in the process as any author could want.

Neither OpSail Maine 2000 nor its education program, of

which this book is very much a part, could have been possible without the cooperation of a dedicated board of directors. In particular, I would like to acknowledge and thank William G. Waldron and the Waldron Group for their generous contribution, which made publication of this book possible. Our thanks also go to Stephen Spenlinhauer and Spencer Press, who donated the paper needed to print this book.

On a personal note, I thank Allison for her unflagging support, and our daughters Kai and Madeleine, to whom I dedicate this book.

Lincoln P. Paine
Portland, Maine
16 April 2000

DOWN EAST

A Maritime History of Maine

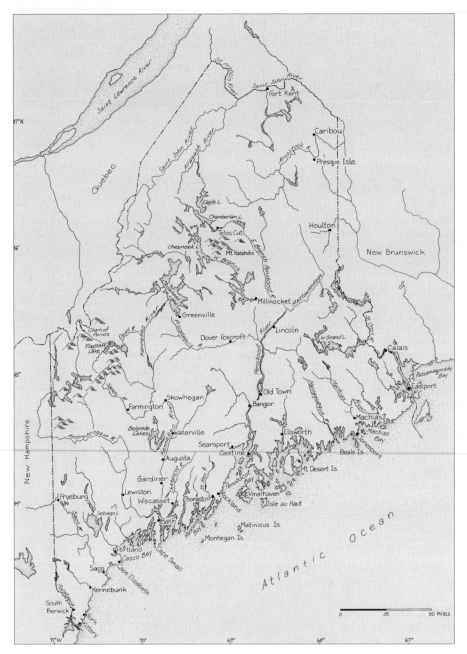

Map of Maine by Rosemary Mosher.

A Sense of Place

LONG BEFORE interstates and Internets, tall ships weaving a worldwide web of international trade made the state of Maine famous the world over. During the 1800s, the heyday of the merchant sailing ship, the names of Maine seaports graced the transoms of handsome square-riggers from Canton to Cape Town, and towns such as Searsport and Kennebunk were as well known and respected as the United States itself. Navigating across thousands of miles of open ocean in an age when time was measured not in minutes but months, sea commerce required skills, stamina, and patience unimaginable to generations for whom e-commerce entails only a click of a mouse on a computer screen. Ship owning was a vital and conspicuous trait of the people of Maine. In 1880, for example, Searsport had a population of only 2,322 people, but it is estimated that 10 percent of all the sailing ship masters in the United States hailed from this modest town on the shores of Penobscot Bay.

Maine's maritime enterprise was by no means confined to long-distance trades. From the upland forests through the long river valleys to the deeply indented, island-speckled coast, Mainers of all stripes have been indebted to the sea—and the Gulf of Maine in particular—for their livelihood. So far as we know, the deliberate use of Maine's lakes, rivers, and coastal waterways began with the development of dugouts and, much later, birchbark canoes. While there is a great deal of partisan feeling about whether the lobster boat, the gaff-rigged schooner, or the towering Down Easter best symbolizes the longstanding traditions of the Maine shipwright, the Maine boat par excellence is in fact the birchbark canoe—and its direct descendants made of aluminum and synthetic fibers. It has been around the longest, been produced in the greatest numbers, and it owes its development to the unique topography of Maine and the waters that wash its 300-mile coastline.

* * *

On a map, the coast of Maine appears to hang like a raveled sleeve of geological time fraying into the cold waters of the Gulf of Maine. The coast—that invisible boundary line between land and sea—is only 293 miles from Kittery to Eastport. Trace the more detailed shoreline where the land and salt water meet, and your journey will take you some 5,000 miles. This helps explain why there are sixty-three lighthouses along the coast—more than in any other state on the East Coast—to guide mariners to safe harbor amid the tendrils of rock and island in the Gulf of Maine.

On the landward side, the Gulf of Maine is bounded by Cape Cod to the south; by Massachusetts, New Hampshire, Maine, and New Brunswick (Canada) to the west and north; and by Nova Scotia to the northeast. The Gulf's submarine boundaries constitute what the U.S. Geological Survey describes as "one of the most striking topographic features off the east coast of the United States," although these are less obvious on most maps. To the south and southwest, the Georges Bank (northeast of Cape Cod) and Browns Bank (southwest of Nova Scotia) separate the Gulf from the Atlantic Ocean and the warm waters of the Gulf Stream (so named for the Gulf of Mexico). A mere 13,000 years ago, towards the end of the last ice age, these Banks were dry extensions of what are now Cape Cod and Nova Scotia. The Gulf of Maine was connected to the Atlantic only by the narrow cut of the Northeast Channel, which flows between the Georges and Browns Banks. When the ice age ended, melting water carved the river valleys more sharply into the landscape, and the rising sea level covered the exposed Banks and filled in the bays along the coast. Today, the average depth of the Gulf is less than 500 feet (150 meters) and that of the Georges Bank less than 200 feet, while the Northeast Channel (22 miles south to north and 38 miles east to west) has a maximum depth of more than 1,200 feet (375 meters).

The geology of Maine consists largely of relatively soft metamorphic rock, harder granite, and in the northeast, rock formed millions of years ago by volcanic eruptions. Geologists divide the coast of Maine into four distinct geological compartments, each

Marsden Hartley's *Maine Coast at Vinalhaven* (1938–39) captures the dominant elements of Midcoast Maine: granite, sea, pine, and sky.
COURTESY BOWDOIN COLLEGE MUSEUM OF ART, BRUNSWICK

of which has given rise to distinct industries and lifestyles among the people who live there. The southern coast, starting at the Piscataqua River (the border between Maine and New Hampshire), is a region of metamorphic rock tipped by granite and shaped in a curved coastline as far as Cape Elizabeth; there are prominent harbors at Kittery, York Harbor, and Kennebunkport. Long ranks of peninsulas and islands shaped from metamorphic rock dominate the indented shoreline of the coast from the Portland region northeast across Casco Bay to Cape Small and from there to Penobscot Bay. On the landward side, this stretch of Midcoast Maine is etched by some of Maine's largest rivers—the Androscoggin, Kennebec, Sheepscot, and St. George, and Muscongus Bay. Of this coast, from Casco Bay to Penobscot Bay, wrote John Smith in 1616, there "is nothing but such high craggy Cliffy Rocks and stony Iles, that I wondered such great trees could growe upon so hard foundations. It is a Countrie to affright, then delight one."

Between Penobscot Bay and Machias Bay lies a region geologists call "islands and bays of Maine," an area of large, widely spaced granite islands such as Vinalhaven, Isle au Haut, and Mount Desert. These enclose stretches of water with such picturesque names as Eggemoggin Reach, the Fox Islands Thorofare, Blue Hill and Frenchman Bays, and Somes Sound, the only fjord on the east coast of North America. About halfway along the coast of Maine, the vast triangle of Penobscot Bay—about 20 miles across and 40 miles deep—takes its name from the river that flows out of the largest drainage basin in the state. The easternmost part of the coast is the cliffed coast, also known as the Sunrise Coast. Lying between Machias Bay and West Quoddy Head on the Canadian border (which runs through Passamaquoddy Bay), this is one of the most exposed and most sparsely settled regions of Down East Maine, a cultural region that runs from Mount Desert Island to Eastport. Forming the southwestern shore of the Bay of Fundy, the tides here rise and fall twenty feet—more than double the range of tide at Kittery.

Unlike terrestrial ecosystems, which tend to have greater bio-logical diversity in warmer climates such as equatorial rainforests, marine ecosystems generally become more diverse as the water temperature decreases. The Gulf of Maine is dominated by the cold waters of the Nova Scotia Current, which flows counter-clockwise from the southern tip of Nova Scotia along the coast of Maine to Massachusetts Bay. The long hook of Cape Cod forces the current east and then north where it runs parallel to the clockwise flow of the Gulf Stream. Surface water temperatures in the Gulf of Maine range from a minimum of about 2°–4°C (36°–39°F) in the winter to a high of about 12°–14°C (54°–57°F) in the summer, the inshore waters being colder than those offshore. Another major factor in the Gulf's ecosystem is the runoff from the approximately sixty rivers that annually dis-charge an estimated 250 billion gallons of fresh water into the Gulf of Maine, much of it spring runoff from melting snow. This snowmelt is rich in nutrients in the form of minerals and decay-ing plants that form the basis of a "plankton soup" that circu-lates within the confines of the Gulf. The estuaries where fresh and salt water meet comprise extremely fertile salt marshes, sea grass and seaweed beds, and intertidal zones.

The majority of the Gulf of Maine estuaries are found within the borders of the state of Maine. The most significant are: on the Southern Coast, Great Bay (at the mouth of the Piscataqua River), Saco and Casco Bays; in the Midcoast region, Merry-meeting,* Sheepscot, Muscongus, and Penobscot Bays; and Down East, Blue Hill, Frenchman, Narraguagus, Machias, and Passamaquoddy Bays. The natural fertility of these regions makes them a magnet for animals from all parts of the food chain, from plankton to shellfish, fish, birds, and mammals, including humans.

* Merrymeeting Bay is so called because it is the confluence of six rivers: An-droscoggin, Kennebec, Eastern, Muddy, Cathance, and Abagadasset. The lower Kennebec (sometimes called the Sagadahoc) resumes its course in solitary splen-dor to enter the Gulf of Maine between Cape Small and Georgetown Island.

For humans, the estuaries provide not only a convenient and stable source of food, but also natural transportation corridors both along the coast and into the interior. Maine is the most heavily forested state in the United States—almost 90 percent of the land is covered in forest, a total of 17.5 million acres. These forests provide shelter and habitat for a large number of animal species. Before the arrival of Europeans, they were also home to various bands of Abnaki—"People of the Dawnland," or easterners—who took their names from the rivers along which they lived, such as the Penobscot and Androscoggin. The area of what is now northeastern Maine was home to the Passamaquoddy, whose territory extended into New Brunswick. Collectively, the various tribes and bands of northern New England and the western Maritime Provinces of Canada called themselves Wabanaki, and they spoke dialects of the Algonquian language.

The chief occupations of the Abnaki were farming, hunting, and fishing and trading along the many rivers and lakes of interior Maine. Light but strong, their canoes could be paddled along very shallow lakes, rivers, and estuaries, and easily portaged between navigable streams. The Penobscot word for canoe was *agwiden*, meaning "floats lightly." Once afloat, the Abnaki were able to develop intricate trade routes that made extensive use of the more than 5,000 lakes and ponds and the hundreds of rivers of interior Maine and as far afield as Quebec and the Bay of Chaleur in the Gulf of St. Lawrence. In recent years, there has been a concerted effort to rediscover their long-dormant trade routes such as the Eastern Maine Canoe Trail, which begins at Vanceboro on the Canadian border and continues for 130 miles of rivers and lakes to the Passadumkeag River and from there into the Penobscot. A sense of the antiquity of this route is clear from a 1920 history of Hinckley Township, in which Minnie Atkinson described the portage used by Passamaquoddy travelers going from the St. Croix River valley west along Grand Lake Stream:

SOMETIMES as many as 20 families would paddle up through the lakes, one family in a canoe, one canoe behind another a long, silent, single line. When the travelers reached the head of Big Lake if they were going still further they would carry the canoes, inverted over the heads and resting on the shoulders of the men, along the east bank of Grand Lake Stream to Grand Lake. An Indian carry, so much used that even the rocks are worn, was thus made across the corner of the township.

Abnaki travel was by no means limited to inland waters. Both birchbark and dugout canoes were quite capable of work on salt water. In summer, in larger canoes and using bows, arrows, and harpoons, they hunted seals, porpoise, and larger whales in the Gulf of Maine, and before the coming of Europeans, Micmacs of Nova Scotia carried copper ingots by sea from the Bay of Fundy across the Gulf of Maine to Massachusetts Bay to trade with the people of Cape Cod. Following his exploration of the coast

Photographed in 1923, "Sunset at Umsaskis Lake" shows a scene that has been repeated countless times in the past 500 years or more.
COURTESY MAINE HISTORICAL SOCIETY, PORTLAND

of Massachusetts in 1603, Martin Pring wrote of the canoes he encountered:

> THEIR BOATS, whereof we brought one to Bristoll, were in proportion like a Wherrie of the Riuer of Thames, seventeene foot long and foure foot broad, made of the Barke of a Birch-tree, farre exceeding in bignesse those of England: it was sowed together with strong and tough Oziers or twigs, and the seames couered ouer with Rozen or Turpentine little inferiour in sweetnesse to Frankincense…: it was also open like a Wherrie, and sharpe at both ends, sauing that the beake was a little bending roundly vpward. And though it carried nine men standing vpright, yet it weighed not at the most aboue sixtie pounds in weight, a thing almost incredible in regard of the largenesse and capacitie thereof. Their Oares were flat at the end…, made of Ash or Maple very light and strong, abot two yards long, wherewith they row very swiftly.

Fishing weirs, such as these photographed at Sandy Island near Eastport, have been used on the Maine coast since well before Europeans first settled here in the 1600s.
COURTESY MAINE HISTORICAL SOCIETY, PORTLAND

Three years later, James Rosier—"a gentleman employed in the voyage" of Captain George Waymouth—penned *A True Relation* of his experiences on the Maine coast. He, too, was impressed with the Abnaki canoes, particularly their speed: "...they in their Canoa with three oares, would at their will go ahead of vs and about vs, when we rowed with eight oars strong; such was their swiftnesse, by reason of the lightnesse and artificiall composition of their Canoa and oares."

Fishing—including ice fishing—was done year-round, but the most important season was the spring, when the Abnaki gathered at the falls and rapids of major rivers to catch salmon, smelt, shad, and bass as they made their way upstream to spawn. In addition to spear fishing, the Abnaki used fishnets and weirs, a type of fence driven into the bed of shallow rivers or bays to corral fish. The Kenduskeag River, a tributary of the Penobscot that flows through Bangor, takes its name from a Maliseet word meaning "eel-weir place." The construction of fish weirs, which predate the Abnaki, was extremely labor-intensive and also used vast quantities of wood. On the whole, though, Abnaki use of timber resources was minimal. Their longhouses were made of bent saplings covered with bark, and their portable wigwams of wooden poles covered with animal hides. Many of their tools, and of course their canoes, were made of wood, but large-scale exploitation of the forests did not occur until the arrival of European settlers in the 1600s.

Two

The European Discovery of Maine

THE PERIOD following Christopher Columbus's first transatlantic voyage from Spain to the Caribbean in 1492 is often described as the Age of Discovery. The best-known aspect of European exploration in the 1500s is the drive to find a direct route to the sources of the lucrative spice trade in the Spice Islands south of the Philippines. The long-distance voyages around the tip of southern Africa, South America, and in search of the Northeast Passage across the top of the Eurasian continent, or the Northwest Passage across North America, were dramatic efforts and are fairly well documented. To a degree, this is because these voyages were either sanctioned or funded by one or another European government. European princes supported these undertakings in part because of a series of agreements that divided the world's newly discovered lands between Portugal and Spain. The most important of these documents was the Treaty of Tordesillas (1494), under which Spain was granted title to all newly discovered lands west of a longitudinal line drawn 370 leagues (about 1,200 miles) west of the Azores and Cape Verde Islands; Portugal received lands east of that line. In reality, Portugal's attention focused on India, the Spice Islands, and Brazil, while the Spanish concerned themselves with South and Central America and Mexico. Apart from a relatively few isolated settlements strung from Florida to Texas, and west to California, the Spanish never established a significant presence north of Mexico. Although the treaty remained in force until 1750, Spain's inability to enforce its provisions left the way open to French, and later English, Dutch, and Swedish explorers and colonists.

Two years after Columbus's epochal voyage, England's Henry VII issued letters patent (in essence, a contract) to John Cabot, "a citizen of Venice" though like Columbus a Genoese by birth, "to seeke out, discover, and finde, by whatsoever iles, countreyes, regions, or provinces of the heathen and infidelis, whiche before this time have beene unbeknownen to all Christians." In 1497 Cabot sailed west from Bristol, England's second-largest port, and crossed to what is now Newfoundland or possibly Nova Scotia. Although he returned with little to show for his efforts, his report so impressed the English that the next year he sailed in command of five ships on a second voyage. One of these vessels turned back early on, but the fate of the other ships and their crews is unknown. Cabot may have reached North America and sailed further south than he had on his first voyage, or he and his men may have perished in mid-ocean.

A quarter century after Cabot, Francis I sponsored France's first voyage of exploration to North America. Sailing in *La Dauphine*, Giovanni da Verrazano (who also had the backing of French silk merchants) cruised the east coast of North America from Florida to Newfoundland in search of a northwest passage to the Orient. In 1524 he and his crew landed at Cape Fear, North Carolina, in New York Bay, Narragansett Bay (near Newport, Rhode Island), and then among the Abnaki on Casco Bay. From there they worked their way east along the coast. At the Penobscot River, Verrazano recorded the name "Oranbega," an Abnaki term that describes a stretch of water between two sets of rapids. Europeans corrupted this to Norumbega, a name later applied to a non-existent city on the Penobscot and, eventually, the whole region now known as New England. He continued east to Cape Breton and Newfoundland before returning to France.

Less than a year after Verrazano's return, Estevan Gomez visited Maine in the course of an exploration from north to south along the coast. Gomez was a Portuguese mariner in Spanish pay who had abandoned Ferdinand Magellan's effort to circumnavigate the globe (1519–21) at the Strait of Magellan on the grounds that there had to be an easier route to the east. Gomez's efforts can be traced in two maps, dating from 1529 and 1545. These make it clear that he investigated the coast in greater detail than had his predecessors. Sailing past Mount Desert, he threaded his way through Eggemoggin Reach, sailed up the Penobscot to the head of navigation (Bangor), and stayed close enough inshore to give names (Spanish, and no longer used) to Pemaquid, Boothbay, the Kennebec, and Casco Bay, among other features. Impressive though they were, Gomez's efforts came to nothing. The reason is simple: the known riches of Central and South America were more attractive than the uncertainty of North America. As the Italian historian Peter Martyr wrote in 1530: "It is to the southward, not the icy north, that everyone in search of a fortune should turn, for below the equator everything is rich."

Although Jacques Cartier's three voyages of exploration to the St. Lawrence River in the 1530s and 1540s showed some promise, for a variety of reasons, neither the English nor the French were able systematically to capitalize on the efforts expended in the first half century of European voyages to North America. Yet merchants and princes were not the only ones drawn to the western Atlantic. Although Cabot returned from his first voyage with neither silks nor precious metals nor spices, he and his men were evidently impressed by the abundance of fish off Newfoundland. According to a letter by Raimondo di Soncino dated 18 December 1497:

...THEY AFFIRM that the sea is covered with fish which are caught not merely with nets but with baskets, a stone being attached to make the basket sink in the water, and this I heard the said Master [Cabot] relate. And said Englishmen, his companions, say that they will fetch so many fish that this kingdom will have no more need of Iceland, from which country there comes a very great store of fish which are called stock-fish.

The profitability of the long-distance fishing industry was due to the importance of fish in the European diet. Dried or salted fish was less expensive than meat, and Church prohibitions against eating meat on fast days—in all, about half the days of the year—led to an increased demand across western Europe. The English government also came to regard the fisheries as "a nursery for seamen"—that is, a good place for sailors to practice their skills in the event they were needed to man ships in wartime. To that end, in 1563 the English Parliament indirectly subsidized the industry by making Wednesdays and Saturdays fish days.

Fish were cured in a number of ways. The easiest was simply to tie two fish together by their tails and sling them over a pole (*stok*, in Dutch) to dry. Fish cured in this way were known as stockfish. If one had no salt—and most northern Europeans had little or no salt suitable for the purpose—this was the only way to cure fish, if the weather was cold and dry enough. The Spanish, Portuguese, and French all had ample supplies of salt, and they cured their fish by salting and drying. The English, whose climate enabled them to make some salt, but not enough for their purposes, developed a compromise method of lightly salting and drying their fish.

Unlike herring, cod has almost no fat, as a result of which it is easily cured and long-lasting. The cod that fishermen followed was the Atlantic cod (*Gadus morhua*), a species found throughout the North Atlantic. A voracious bottom dweller that devours other fish, shellfish, and squid whole, the cod is found at depths of between 120 feet and 900 feet (20 to 150 fathoms) in water about 47°F (8°C), so they migrate with the change of the seasons, usually not much more than 100 miles in either direction and at a slow pace, about three miles a day. Although cod populations have now been severely overfished, 400 years ago enormous cod weighing as much as 200 pounds and measuring six feet in length were not uncommon.

The abundance of cod in the Gulf of Maine, and especially along the coast, is a fact stressed time and again in the *Relations*

The schematic map shows the relative position of the major fishing banks in the Gulf of Maine and the western Atlantic.
MAP BY ROSEMARY MOSHER

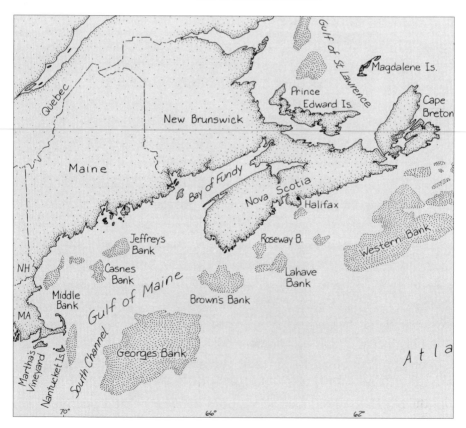

written by participants in English voyages made between 1602 and 1608. Following his trip to Maine with the Waymouth expedition in 1605, James Rosier, one of the more literate and observant pamphleteers of English exploration, remarked several times on the ease with which fish could be caught. Cruising among the islands at the entrance to the St. George River in Muscongus Bay,

WHILE WE thus sounded from one place to another in so good deepes, our Captaine to make some triall of the fishing himselfe, caused a hooke or two to be cast out at the mouth of the harbor, not aboue halfe a league from our ship, where in small time only, with the baits which they cut

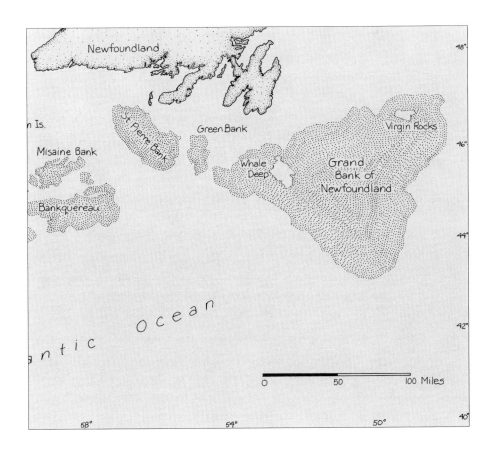

from the fish and three hooks, we got fish enough for our whole Company (though now augmented) for three daies. Which I omit not to report, because it sheweth how great a profit the fishing would be, they being so plentifull, so great, and so good, with such conuenient drying as can be wished, neere at hand vpon the Rocks.

In the Middle Ages, Baltic and North Sea herring were the staple food fish of Western Europe. Monopolistic control by merchants of the Hanseatic League coupled with a partial collapse of the herring fishery led to the opening of the Icelandic cod fisheries, and by the early 1300s, English ports regularly sent vessels to fish for cod in the waters off Iceland. News of Cabot's voyage to new fishing grounds teeming with fish spread quickly, and in 1527 the English navigator John Rut reported seeing fourteen fishing ships in Haven of St. John, Newfoundland, including one from Brittany, eleven from Normandy, and two from Portugal. A Spaniard on the same voyage recorded that they encountered a total of fifty vessels along the coast of Newfoundland. The tensions that arose from such crowding led to a steady search for new fishing grounds that drew European fishermen ever westward from the Grand Banks south of Newfoundland to Nova Scotia and eventually the Gulf of Maine, which the English began to exploit in the early 1600s.

Although there were probably European fishermen in these waters in the late 1500s, it was only after Waymouth's voyage that English fishermen began to establish themselves on the Maine coast. Monhegan Island, off the entrance to Penobscot Bay, became the primary fishing station. Financed by merchants in London and England's West Country ports, other seasonal stations were established on Matinicus, Damariscove, Stratton's Island, Richmond Island, and the Isle of Shoals, and on the mainland at Saint George, New Harbor, Pemaquid, the mouth of the Sagadahoc (Kennebec), Winter Harbor (Saco), and Kittery Point. Although they eventually came to dominate it absolutely, the English were by no means the only people attracted to the Maine fisheries in this period. By the early 1620s, it is estimated that as many as 400 fishing vessels of various nationalities—about 10 percent of them English, including vessels from the James-town Colony in Virginia—fished on the Maine coast each year. In keeping to the islands, which they used chiefly for drying and salting fish, and for repairing their boats, they could avoid en-croaching on rival fishermen or the Abnaki ashore.

Nonetheless, there is abundant evidence of relations between Native Americans and Europeans in this period. In 1602 Bartho-lomew Gosnold anchored his *Concord* in the vicinity of what is now Cape Elizabeth. According to the Reverend John Brereton's account, while at anchor,

> ...EIGHT INDIANS, in a Baske-shallop with mast and saile, an iron grapple, and a kettle of Copper, came boldly abo-ord vs, one of them appareled with a wastcoat and breeches of blacke serge, made after our sea-fashion, hose and shoes on his feet; all the rest (saving one that had a paire of breeches of blue clothe) were naked.

The English learned, from "some signs and words they made," that they had traded with Basque fishermen from the port of Saint Jean de Luz, a French fishing port on the Bay of Biscay. The Indians were also able to draw a map showing the location of the Newfoundland fisheries, some 800 miles to the northeast.

In 1604, at the same time that English activity in Maine was on the increase, the French explorer Samuel de Champlain at-tempted to establish a colony on St. Croix Island in the St. Croix River, along what is now the Canadian border. His purpose was to assess the country, learn about the inhabitants, and establish a colony that would become the center of French fisheries and fur-trapping operations. An indefatigable and disciplined explorer, he mapped the region between Martha's Vineyard and the Bay of Fundy, and he named Petit and Grand Manan Islands, Isle au

Haut, and Mount Desert Island.[*] However, the man known to history as "The father of New France" was shocked by the climate—"There are six months of winter in this country," he despaired—which claimed the lives of thirty-five of his men. As a result, the French left St. Croix for Port Royal (now Annapolis Royal, Nova Scotia). They subsequently focused their energy on establishing settlements in the St. Lawrence River valley where the land was reasonably fertile, near the fishing grounds of the Gulf of St. Lawrence, and the potential for fur trading was limitless. If the English so chose, the way was now open for them to pursue a program of colonization in New England with relatively little interference from European rivals.

[*] As spoken in Maine, Isle au Haut rhymes with Idaho. Isles des Monts Deserts were so called because "The summit of most of them [mountains] is destitute of trees, and there are only rocks on them." The French origin and spelling of the name accounts for the spelling of Desert, which is usually pronounced "dessert."

THREE

The Coming of
the English

SHALLOPS SUCH as Brereton, Champlain, and others mention in their accounts were relatively small, open boats, about 25 to 45 feet long. They were general-purpose boats, which the English and French used for a variety of purposes. The shallop seems to have originated as a ship's boat, and there are many accounts of shallops being carried in pieces aboard ship for assembly at the vessel's destination. A shallop carried in four pieces aboard the *Mayflower* in 1620 was found to be "much bruised and shattered in the ship with foul weather," although after repairs it proved invaluable to the colonists. Most vessels referred to as shallops in the early 1600s were apparently one-masted vessels that set a single square sail and had no deck. Vessels later referred to as shallops were obviously larger, with decks and more complex rigs, sometimes with two masts, and setting a staysail forward.

Another vessel referred to frequently in early records is the pinnace. Although pinnace and shallop are sometimes used interchangeably, the pinnace seems to have been a small vessel in its own right rather than a small boat assigned to a larger ship. It follows that pinnaces tended to be larger than shallops, with high, square sterns, and decked over. Although vessels of the period were usually distinguished by their hull form rather than their rig, one characteristic of the pinnace might have been that they were rigged with fore-and-aft sails, that is, sails set parallel to the centerline of the vessel. (A square sail is set perpendicular to the centerline.) Fore-and-aft rigs are more maneuverable than a square rig and therefore are well suited to work on long, indented coastlines. Despite their relatively small size, it was not unusual for pinnaces to be used for coastal and transatlantic trade. Indeed the first vessel built in Maine by the English for ocean trade was the pinnace *Virginia*, launched into the Kennebec in 1607.

At this time, Virginia (so-called for Elizabeth I, the Virgin Queen), was the English name for all the land from the state of

A replica of the Pilgrims' *Mayflower*, built in England in 1956, towing her shallop astern.
COURTESY PLIMOTH PLANTATION, PLYMOUTH, MASSACHUSETTS

Virginia to New England. Following on voyages of Gosnold and Waymouth, in April 1606 James I chartered the Virginia Company to encourage settlement in this region. South Virginia, the lands between 34° and 41°N, was to be settled by the London division of the Virginia Company. North Virginia, between 38° and 45°N, was granted to the Plymouth division. (The area of overlap—between 38° and 41°N, or from southern Maryland to southern Connecticut—was reserved to whichever division got there first.) The Londoners were first off the mark, and in December 1606 they dispatched the *Susan Constant, Godspeed,* and *Discovery* with the colonists who would establish the Jamestown Colony in what is now the state of Virginia.

In the meantime, Sir John Popham, chief justice of England, his son Sir Francis Popham, and Sir Ferdinando Gorges, Fort Major of Plymouth, were planning a voyage to New England. On May 31, 1607, *Gifte of God* and the *Mary and John* sailed from Plymouth with a complement consisting largely of retired soldiers who were to establish a fort at the mouth of the Kennebec River and develop a fur trade with the Abnaki. Sailing via Nova Scotia, the English arrived at the Kennebec on August 18. Here they built a fort and a man known to history simply as Digby of London began to build a pinnace—the *Virginia*—for exploring upriver. It seems that rather than being assembled from prefabricated sections, the *Virginia* was made entirely of materials gathered in Maine—with the exception of iron fastenings and cordage for the rigging. The only written descriptions of the pinnace state that she was of 30 tons—perhaps 50 feet long. There is a contemporary drawing of Fort St. George that includes a sketch that may depict the *Virginia*.

The *Mary and John* and *Gifte of God* sailed for home during the fall, leaving forty-five colonists to struggle through the winter on the Kennebec. According to court documents, *Gifte of God*'s master, John Havercombe, stopped first in the Azores Islands to "furnish himself and his company with victuals by the sale of [33] masts, [3] spars, and other things." This is the first reference to any exploitation of Maine's timber resources, which would eventually outstrip even the fisheries in importance.

There are no detailed accounts of what happened for the remainder of the colony's existence. Two small ships arrived in May or June of 1608, followed by *Gifte of God* in the early fall. In the meantime, George Popham died and his successor Raleigh Gilbert was returning home to an inheritance. Because there were "no mynes discouered, nor hope thereof," and because of "the feare that all other winters would proue like this first," it was decided to abandon the colony. "Wherefore they all embarqued in that this new arrived shippe and in the new Pynnace ye *Virginia* and sett saile for England, and this was the end of the northerenn Colony yponn the Riuer of Sachadehoc."

With the failure of the "Second Colonie," many of the expedition's backers turned to the London group, which also ac-

John Hunt's picture plan of Fort St. George, at the mouth of the Kennebec River, dated October 8, 1607. The vignette to the left of the fort may be a rendering of the pinnace *Virginia*.
COURTESY MAINE MARITIME MUSEUM, BATH

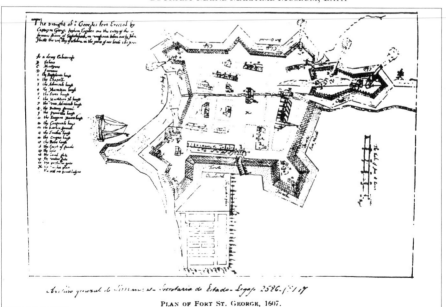

PLAN OF FORT ST. GEORGE, 1607.

Shakespeare and the *"Virginia"*

The pinnace *Virginia* played a bit part in one of literature's best known shipwrecks. In 1609, she was one of two pinnaces and six ships sent by the Virginia Company with supplies for the Jamestown colony. The flagship, *Sea Venture*, was separated from the other vessels in a hurricane and grounded on Bermuda, a place dreaded by mariners. The company of 150 men rowed ashore and built two pinnaces in which they sailed to Jamestown. The shipwreck was the subject of two published accounts, William Strachey's *True Repertory of the Wreck and Redemption of Sir Thomas Gates, Knight,* and Silvester Jourdain's *Discovery of Bermuda otherwise called the "Isle of Devils."* It is believed that William Shakespeare read both these accounts in the course of writing his celebrated romantic drama *The Tempest* (1611), the last of his complete plays.

quired the *Virginia*. She was one of two pinnaces and six ships that formed the "third supply" to Jamestown in the summer of 1609. The ultimate fate of this veteran of at least two transatlantic voyages is not known, though by some accounts she remained in service for twenty years. The venture and its backers are otherwise best remembered in a few place names, notably Fort Gorges at the mouth of Portland's Fore River, and Fort Popham and Popham Beach at the mouth of the Kennebec.

The failure of the Popham Colony put an end to organized efforts to settle Northern Virginia for the time being, but it hardly meant the end of English interest in Maine. Fishermen became even more ensconced, and their shore establishments took on a more permanent character, for there was money to be made. In the early 1620s, a Plymouth merchant by the name of Abraham Jennings took possession of the fishing station at Monhegan, where he loaded for Bordeaux a single shipment of more than

173,000 dried fish (about 170 tons) with a value of about $75,000. There were more or less permanent settlements at Richmond Island off Cape Elizabeth's Crescent Beach and at Damariscove Island near the mouth of the Sheepscot River. One indication of the prosperity of these enclaves is the sort of attention they attracted—from French and other European pirates and from Abnaki raiders, the latter often backed by the French.

The fishing posts were also an important part of the nascent English presence elsewhere in Virginia. They were frequented by fishermen from Jamestown, and after 1622 they were in regular contact with the Pilgrims at Plymouth, Massachusetts. The Plymouth Colony had received its charter from the Council for New England, in essence a reorganized Plymouth branch of the

An illustration showing the primary activities of a fishing station on Newfoundland—not unlike those found on the coast of Maine— from Heinrich Moll's "New and Exact Map of the Dominions...1715."
COURTESY OSHER MAP LIBRARY, PORTLAND.

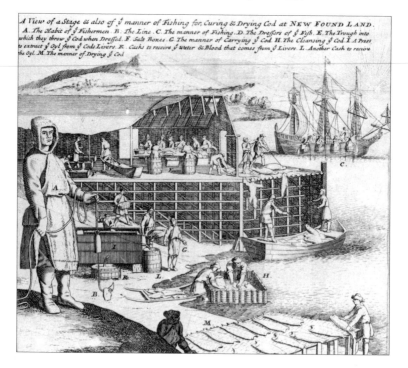

Virginia Company founded in 1620. The Council proved unable to enforce its authority and its powers eventually reverted to the Crown, which issued royal charters to prospective settlers. The Plymouth group's other signal accomplishment was sending John Smith on two voyages to Northern Virginia in 1614–15. Smith was captured by pirates, and during his captivity he wrote *A Description of New England,* the title of which was deliberately calculated to encourage people from old England to settle in North America. "And of all the foure parts of the world that I haue yet seene not inhabited," he wrote, "could I have but meanes to transport a Colonie, I would rather liue here then any where...." As to the naming of Maine, it is said (with less authority) that the name honored Charles I's queen, Henrietta Maria, sister of the king of France and feudal proprietor of the French province of Maine.

Formal settlement in the 1600s was concentrated between the Piscataqua and Presumpscot Rivers, and towns were founded at Saco, Kittery, and most notably, York, briefly known as Gorgeanna (in honor of Sir Ferdinando Gorges). Maine's expanding prosperity slowed somewhat during the English Civil War (1642–46), and in 1652 the territory became subject to Massachusetts, whose Puritan leaders had no sympathy for Royalists like Gorges. Massachusetts bought out his family's claim to lands west of the Kennebec in 1677. Though he had accomplished little of lasting value for himself or his heirs, Sir Ferdinando was probably the most vigorous proponent of English colonization in North America.

FOUR

"For the good and securitie of England"

IF FISH drew Europeans to the coast of Maine, it was the promise of furs and ship timber that lured them inland. Although Champlain had dismissed Maine as an unlivable place, French trappers and fishermen were active east of the Penobscot, and the French had a fort at Pentagoët (Castine) to guard the approaches to the rich trapping grounds in the Penobscot River valley. The importance of this modest fort can be gauged from the fact that in the mid-1600s, when the entire population of French Acadia was perhaps 500, its garrison numbered eighteen.* Trappers were transient by nature, and unlike the English, French fishermen tended to avoid the establishment of anything but temporary fishing stations ashore. As a result, the French had little incentive to establish either towns or government—apart from Pentagoët—south of the St. John River. This, and their willingness to trade guns, enabled them to co-exist with the Abnaki on reasonably amicable terms.

---

* Acadia was a corruption of Arcadia, the name Verrazano had given the region in an allusion to a part of Ancient Greece renowned for its rustic bliss.

The same could not be said of the English in western Maine. In his *Description of New England*, Smith promised prospective settlers that they might find "fishing before your doors, may every night sleep quietly ashore with good cheare and what fires you will, or when you please with your wives and familie." This was a marked departure from the seasonal, island-based approach to fishing that then prevailed, and one that quickly altered the basis of English relations with the Abnaki. Tensions were aggravated by the fact that the English colonists were voracious consumers of wood—for construction and shipbuilding in the colonies, for export to the Caribbean and the British Isles, or simply clearing land for farms and towns. The search for the best stands of timber drew them steadily inland and they encroached more heavily on Abnaki lands.

So far as the English were concerned, one of the longstanding attractions of North America generally and New England in particular was the ready availability of ship timber, especially trees suitable for masts. Their own domestic supply of useful trees had been all but exhausted, and England relied on Baltic sources for naval stores of all sorts, including masts and tar. (Tar was used as a preservative for rigging.) A treatise first published in the 1590s and "containing important inducements" for settlement in North America stressed that:

> IT MAY ALSO be a matter of great consequence for the good and securitie of England; that out of these Northerly regions we shall be able to furnish this realme of all manner of prouisions for our nauies; namely, Pitch, Rosen, Cables, Ropes, Masts, and such like.

The Popham Colony had exported a shipload of masts that were sold in the Azores in 1608, and the following year Henry Hudson stopped at the southern end of Penobscot Bay to cut and step a new foremast for the *Halve Maen*. The first cargo of masts was exported from Penobscot Bay to England in the 1630s, but the New England mast trade got its real start during the first

Anglo-Dutch War in the 1650s, when the Danish fleet closed the Baltic to English shipping. In 1685 the Crown imposed some order on the business by appointing a Surveyor of Pine and Timber, the intent being to reserve for the Royal Navy the biggest trees available—the largest could measure 38 inches in diameter at the base and 115 feet tall. Six years later, Massachusetts Bay was issued a new charter by which Maine was made a province of the colony, and:

> ...FOR THE better providing and furnishing of Masts for our Royal Navy wee do hereby reserve to us, our heirs and successors all trees of the diameter of twenty-four inches and upwards at twelve inches from the ground, growing upon any Soils or Tract of Land within our said Province or Territory not heretofore granted to any private Persons.

The trees in question, white pine or *Pinus strobus,* were marked with the "broad arrow"—three strokes of an axe in the form of a barbed arrowhead or crow's foot to indicate that they belonged to the king. After 1729 the law reserved for the Royal Navy all white pine not privately owned, regardless of size, from Nova Scotia to New Jersey.

Located at the mouth of the Piscataqua River across from Kittery, Portsmouth, New Hampshire, was the original center of the navy's mast trade. In time there were also significant operations at Falmouth (Portland), Freeport, and Georgetown. Whenever possible, timber was harvested near rivers deep enough to float the logs. Failing that, the trees were felled and "baulked" overland to the nearest stream by huge teams of as many as one hundred oxen. Winter was the season to cut trees because the ground was hard and if the rivers were frozen, the logs could be left on the ice until the spring thaw. The high water of the spring floods meant fewer shallows and less likelihood of damage to the masts. In the days before mechanized transport, these were common practices throughout the timber industry, whether for mast trees or any others.

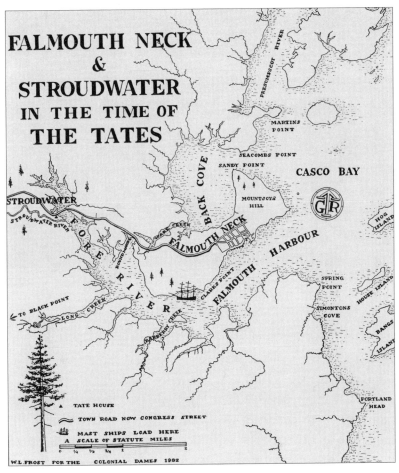

"Falmouth Neck and Stroudwater in the Time of the Tates."
COURTESY TATE HOUSE, PORTLAND

Floated downstream, the logs were collected at mast landings until they could be roughly shaped and loaded on ships specially designed for the purpose. Such craft had special ports in the stern so that the timbers, which were nearly as long as the ships that carried them, could be slid into the hull. The largest trees available from Baltic sources measured only 30 inches in diameter, and the mast ships designed for that trade usually measured about 200 to 400 tons burden. Owing to the immense size of

Masts were loaded into ships through special ports cut in the hull, as
seen in this diorama depicting the mast trade at Falmouth.
COURTESY TATE HOUSE, PORTLAND

the New England mast trees—the heaviest were more than 20
tons—mast ships in the American trade measured 400 to 600
tons, and as big as 1,000 tons burden, the size of a large warship.* The importance of New England masts in the seventeenth
and eighteenth centuries has been likened to that of oil in the
twentieth and twenty-first centuries, an apt comparison as is suggested in the relieved diary entry of naval administrator Samuel
Pepys in 1666, during the second Anglo-Dutch War:

> THERE IS ALSO the very good newes comes of four New
> England ships come home safe to Falmouth [England]
> with masts for the King; which is a blessing mighty unex-
> pected, and without which, if for nothing else, we must
> have failed the next year. But God be praised for thus much
> good fortune, and send up the continuance of his favor in
> other things! So to bed.

---

* Ship tonnage is a measure of volume (roughly equivalent to 100 cubic feet),
rather than of weight (2,000 pounds).

Because mast trees could fetch such high prices—a white pine 36 inches in diameter sold for £135 in 1664 and £153 a century later—there was strong incentive to buy and harvest forestland in Maine. As the English became more established, cultural differences led to increased friction between the colonists and the Abnaki. Occasional skirmishes erupted into open warfare for the first time during King Philip's War. The conflict started in 1675 in Massachusetts—King Philip was the English name for Metacomet, a Wampanoag sachem—as a reaction to the colonists' expansion. Fighting swept over most of New England, but ended formally soon after Philip's death in 1676. In Maine, hostilities continued until 1678, by which time the Abnaki had driven the English off the land east of the Kennebec, including many of the islands, and they had destroyed the towns of Casco and Scarborough. Trade, which now included furs and wood products such as boards, shingles, clapboards, barrel staves, oars, anchor stocks, and house frames came to an end. Fishing in the Gulf of Maine was severely disrupted by Abnaki raiders and French privateers. In the summer of 1677, an Abnaki leader named Mugg led a campaign that led to the capture of more than twenty fishing boats and their crews. According to the testimony of an English settler captured by the Abnaki, Mugg intended to lead a full-scale invasion of Boston in ships captured from the fishing fleet. Whether he could have found the crews necessary for such an undertaking is debatable. In any event, Mugg was killed during a raid on Black Point, near Richmond Island, and the plan was never realized.

King Philip's War was the first in a series of conflicts that pitted English colonists against Native Americans, usually supported by French Acadia. Between the 1630s and 1763, the English and French vied halfheartedly for control of Maine, which they intended to divide between themselves. The border shifted several times as the result of peace treaties negotiated in Europe. The Treaty of St. Germain (1632), for example, set the border at the Penobscot River. The Treaty of Ryswick (1697) moved the border—south and west to the Kennebec River, according to the

French interpretation, or north and east to the St. Croix River (the modern border between Maine and New Brunswick) according to the English.

Diplomats in Europe were one thing, but daily life in Maine was quite another, subject to the initiative or whim of soldiers and settlers. Pentagoët, in particular, was a frequent victim of naval forces or privateers with nothing better to do. In 1654 the British garrison in Boston was ordered to seize the Dutch colony of New Amsterdam (New York). The unanticipated end to the first Anglo-Dutch War upset the plans of a Major Robert Sedgwick, so he decided "to spend a lyttle time rangeing the coast against the French." Between July and September, Sedgwick seized the French settlements at St. John, Port Royal, and Pentagoët. Acadia remained under loose English control until 1670.

Four years later, the town fell prey to one Jurrien Aernouts. This Dutch West Indies-based captain was originally commissioned to sail against New York (which the Dutch had surrendered to the English in 1664) only to find upon his arrival that the second Anglo-Dutch War had ended. With the encouragement of a Boston merchant, Aernouts decided to raid French holdings Down East. Opposition was slight, and after forcing the surrender of Pentagoët, Machias, and St. John, he optimistically declared the territory between the Penobscot and St. John Rivers the Province of New Holland, and waited for reinforcements from home. These never materialized, and New Holland never amounted to more than a haven for the piratical remnants of Aernouts's crew, who were captured and brought to trial at Boston in 1675.

Although colonial Maine and the rest of New England rebounded after King Philip's War, improvements came largely at the expense of the Abnaki and other Native Americans. These tensions were aggravated by the poor relations between England and France as each sought to gain the support of native peoples in and between their respective overseas holdings. The uneasy peace in North America lasted barely a decade. It was broken by

King William's War,[*] which took place over a wide territory that extended as far as Hudson's Bay. Hostilities in Maine were concentrated along the coast between Kittery and Castine. By the end of 1690, when the white population was still no more than 2,000, the Abnaki had destroyed Berwick and Falmouth, and forced the colonists to abandon their holdings east of Wells. At the same time, Sir William Phipps led an expedition of eight ships which captured Port Royal and destroyed the fortifications there. Phipps left the town under French rule after the inhabitants took an oath to William and Mary, and the same summer he led a large force of 32 ships and 2,200 soldiers against Montreal, with conspicuously less success.[**] Privateering was widespread in the Gulf of Maine throughout the war, and the trade and fisheries upon which both the English and the French depended was disrupted. When peace came—with the French in 1697 and the Abnaki in 1699—the map remained unchanged, but the mutual mistrust was more deeply ingrained.

Southern Maine was relatively unscathed in the conflict, and shipwrights on the Piscataqua undertook the construction of the first two ships built for the Royal Navy in the colonies, and the start (albeit a tentative one) of a tradition of naval shipbuilding in Maine that continues today. Launched at Langdon's (Badger) Island in 1695, the 48-gun, fourth-rate frigate HMS *Falkland* (638 tons, 129 feet) was built by a timber merchant named John Holland on speculation for the Royal Navy, which purchased the

---

[*] French and Indian Wars is the name given to a series of conflicts fought in North America between 1689 and 1763. As each was essentially an American theater of an Anglo-French conflict, they have both colonial and European names: King William's War/War of the League of Augsburg (1689–97), Queen Anne's War/War of the Spanish Succession (1702–13), King George's War/War of the Austrian Succession (1744–48), and French and Indian War/Seven Years' War (1755/56–1763).

[**] One of America's first rags-to-riches stories, the Woolwich-born Phipps began life as a shipwright's apprentice. He was knighted—the first native-born American so honored—for his role in the discovery of a shipwreck that netted him £30,000, and he later became the first royal governor of Massachusetts, including his native Maine.

ship the next year. In 1697 the 32-gun *Bedford Galley* (373 tons, 103 feet) was built on New Castle Island by a Mr. Taylor and purchased just after completion. Colonial vessels at this time were often built of green (unseasoned) wood, which made them susceptible to rot. This may account for the fact that the *Falkland* had to be rebuilt in England in 1702. She remained in service until 1718; the *Bedford Galley* was broken up in 1709. There was also a tendency for people in England to deprecate colonial workmanship, but whatever the reason, no other vessels were built for the Royal Navy in the American colonies for fifty years.

Although these were the first warships built in the colonies, boat- and shipbuilding was a well-established profession by the 1690s. Records show that between 1693 and 1714, Kittery and York turned out forty-seven vessels of 30 tons burden or more.

An undated photograph showing two men whipsawing planks at the Charles Ward Shipyard on the Kennebunk River.
COURTESY BRICK STORE MUSEUM, KENNEBUNK

William Phipps began his career as an apprentice shipwright in Boston before establishing his own shipyard at Woolwich on Montsweag Bay in the 1670s. During King Philip's War, a large number of settlers from the surrounding area fled to his yard and escaped on a merchant vessel he had just built. Smaller vessels had always been needed for moving goods and people along the coast and up the rivers, and there was also a demand for fishing boats for the inshore and offshore fisheries. Colonial shipwrights and seamen received a big boost at mid-century when the Navigation Acts required that most goods destined for either England or the colonies be carried in vessels built in England or the colonies, and manned by English crews, colonials included. At the same time, trade between Maine and Massachusetts, and with other North American and West Indian colonies, was expanding rapidly. Before the 1700s, the demand for ships to satisfy expanding opportunities outstripped the shortage of skilled labor, the need for which was acute. As one historian of American shipbuilding has written:

> SAWING PLANK was a laborious process. A pit was dug and a staging set up across it, the log was levered out on the staging and sawn by the use of a long two-man handsaw.... One man stood on the staging, astraddle the log and facing opposite to the direction of the saw-cut. The man in the pit faced the direction of the saw-cut, to avoid sawdust, and by alternately pulling on the saw, the men could rip a log into a plank. The work was slow and required so much work that the "sawyer" became a recognized trade.

Sawmills were a vastly more efficient alternative to the handsaw—in the seventeenth century, the smallest could cut as much wood as twenty sawyers—but they required reliable sources of waterpower. The first such mill in New England was built at York or Berwick in 1634, and by 1706 there were seventy mills on the Piscataqua alone. Shipbuilding was centered on rivers with strong currents or where water could be caught in pools to create tide mills. The sawmills existed to cut raw timber into staves, shingles, and planks for export, so it was logical and convenient to build ships at or near the same mills that produced their cargoes, and these were found from Kittery to the Kennebec. Significant shipbuilding farther east did not begin until the mid-1700s.

Shipbuilding also went hand-in-hand with both fishing and trade. The origin of Maine's first great merchant family, the Pepperells of Kittery Point, is a case in point. Born near Plymouth, England, William Pepperell got his start in the Isle of Shoals fishery in the 1670s. A man of uncommon enterprise and ambition, he acquired shares in a number of vessels, and with the proceeds from these set himself up on the mainland in nearby Kittery. There he married the daughter of a local shipwright. Maintaining his interest in the fisheries, he expanded into boatbuilding and trade. Pepperell's move ashore coincided with a dramatic change in the fisheries. As the center of the shoreside enterprise moved from the islands to the mainland, especially Salem and Gloucester in Massachusetts, vessels grew in size and New England fishermen began venturing onto the Grand Banks off Newfoundland. As a result, Newfoundland quickly became an important market for New England traders and shipbuilders, and it remained one until after the American Revolution. Most of the trade was legitimate, but Newfoundland was also an important market for goods smuggled in defiance of the Navigation Acts.

Although the Navigation Acts certainly brought some benefit to New England, they were a mixed blessing for merchants. Virtually all European goods imported into the colonies had first to be "laid on the shores of England"—that is, unloaded and reloaded. This re-exportation caused unnecessary delays, drove up the handling costs, and resulted in the imposition of double duties on some goods—for import to and export from England! Important exceptions were salt, for curing fish, and wine and fruit from the Azores and Madeira. Exports were also controlled and certain "enumerated" goods could be exported only to England. Although few of these originated in Maine—by 1776 only furs, masts, and naval stores were included—the Navigation Acts nonetheless inhibited the activities of Maine merchants shipping cargoes from other colonial ports—Virginia tobacco, for example. As the list of enumerated goods grew, so did the volume of goods smuggled.

The North American colonies had been all but ignored during the English Civil Wars of the 1640s, when New England merchants were forced to carve out new markets for themselves. They chafed under new restrictions imposed from London, which not only inhibited the growth of trade but also represented a giant step backward. Many merchants—the Pepperells among them—grew adept at evading or ignoring the law as it suited them, and amassed considerable fortunes in the process. By 1725, when young William joined his father's business, the Pepperell fleet numbered thirty ships engaged in voyages to Newfoundland, the Caribbean, and Europe. The family also owned vast tracts of timberland throughout New Hampshire and Maine.

The rise of the Pepperell and other New England fortunes was carried out against a background of almost continuous warfare between Britain and France. By 1700 most Abnaki were apparently anxious to avoid further confrontation with the colonists, but in 1703 a force of French Canadians and Micmacs twice raided the coast between Wells and Casco Bay. In response, the English declared war on the Maine Indians. Rather than fight, many moved inland, some as far as the St. Lawrence valley. There was little fighting in Maine thereafter, but in 1710 a naval expedition from the Piscataqua succeeded in capturing Port Royal for the last time. Under the Treaty of Utrecht (1713), which ended Queen Anne's War, all of French Acadia (including present-day New Brunswick) and Newfoundland were ceded to Britain; Port Royal became Annapolis Royal.

Isle Royale (now Cape Breton, Nova Scotia) remained part of France, and following the war the French built a fortress at Louisbourg. When war again broke out in 1744, it became a base of privateering operations against English shipping in the Gulf of

Maine. With this direct threat to their livelihood, the colonial government appointed William Pepperell the younger to lead an amphibious expedition against Louisbourg, one of the strongest fortresses in the Americas. In April 1745 Pepperell sailed his fleet of 100 vessels, the majority of them quite small, into Louisbourg Harbor and landed an amphibious force. After a siege, the fort fell on June 16. In recognition of his action, the Maine shipbuilder and merchant was made Baronet Pepperell of Massachusetts.

The rebuilding of abandoned towns and the establishment of new ones after Queen Anne's War had led to the last major confrontation between the English and the Abnaki. Although there was little naval action in the war, except for the customary use of fleets to move soldiers along the coast, by the end of Dummer's War (1721–27) the unity of the coastal Abnaki had been broken, and many had fled inland, some as far as Canada. Opposition to English settlement in southwestern Maine all but disappeared, and although the last Abnaki battles wouldn't be fought until the French and Indian War (1756–63), the coast and major rivers were open to colonial expansion as far as the Penobscot.

The signing of Dummer's Treaty coincided with the appointment of the first Royal Navy mast agent assigned to Stroudwater Landing, at the confluence of the Stroudwater and Fore Rivers in Falmouth (now Portland).* Incorporated in 1717, Falmouth comprised the area of what are now Cape Elizabeth, Westbrook, Falmouth, Portland, and South Portland, although the center of activity—a population of some fifty families in 1720—was on Falmouth Neck, the Portland peninsula. With its large, sheltered harbor on Casco Bay and its situation halfway between the New Hampshire border and the Penobscot, Falmouth quickly became Maine's political, economic, and cultural center. Soon it eclipsed Portsmouth, New Hampshire, in importance for the region, which was also growing at a phenomenal rate.

---

* A stroud was a woolen blanket made especially for trade with Native Americans.

Between 1690 and 1743 the white population of Maine grew six-fold, to about 12,000, and between 1760 and 1790 it roughly doubled every ten years, to 96,000. By 1776 the Abnaki population in Maine was less than 3,000; there was also a small African-American population of fewer than 500, most of them slaves in the southern towns. The only towns with populations over 2,000 were south of Falmouth, which had 3,800 people. The largest in Lincoln County, which then extended from the Kennebec east to the St. Croix, were Georgetown, with 1,700, and Pownalborough, 1,400. In the early 1700s, there had been only twenty-one towns in the province; in the quarter century before the Revolution, 120 new townships were established. Patterns of settlement were determined by navigable water; as had always been the case, virtually all new towns sprang up either on protected bays and coves, or inland along rivers like the Androscoggin, Kennebec, and Penobscot.

Transportation by land was practically impossible. While making the eastern circuit in July 1770, John Adams deplored the conditions of the road near Saco, "their many sharp, steep Hills, many Rocks, many deep Rutts, and not a Footstep of Man, except in the Road. It was vastly disagreeable." Thirty years later, as he penned his autobiography, his memory of the experience remained vivid.

FROM FALMOUTH now Portland in Casco Bay, to Pounalborough There was an entire Wilderness, except North Yarmouth, New Brunswick, and Long reach. The Roads, where a Wheel had never rolled from the Creation, were miry and founderous, incumbered with long Sloughs of Water. The Stumps of the Trees which had been cutt to make the road all remaining fresh and the Roots crossing the path some above ground and some beneath so that my Horses would frequently get between the Roots and he would flounce and blunder, in danger of breaking his own Limbs as well as mine.

For all intents and purposes there were no roads to be found east of the Kennebec. Down East was so remote from the seat of colonial power that in 1763 when a group from Scarborough landed at Machias and sought to obtain a land grant, they mistakenly applied to the colonial government in Nova Scotia rather than the one in Massachusetts. A survivor of the Penobscot Expedition, which took six days to sail from Boston to Penobscot Bay in June 1779, reported that on the overland retreat to the Kennebec, "most of us were six or seven days before we came to an inhabited country." According to Eastport historian Lorenzo Sabine, "A horse was a curiosity and many persons never saw one until 1804."

The new settlements were sometimes named for the Massachusetts towns from which the founders came, such as New Gloucester, New Boston (Gray), and New Marblehead (Windham). Bowdoin, Waldo, Hallowell, and Gardiner and similar town names honored the Massachusetts proprietors on whose land they stood. Despite the stature of local men like Phipps and Pepperell, they were rarities. Most Mainers were frontiersmen eking out a hard living on the margins of the sea or land owned by absentee landlords. The primary professions remained fishing, the timber trades, and shipbuilding. Agricultural output was so meager that for many settlements food shortages were a way of life, and they depended heavily on merchants either based in or with strong commercial ties to Boston. In the more isolated communities, merchants were often despised as greedy outsiders.

Yet coastal and foreign trade worked to the advantage of the smallest communities, too. Even as resistance to British duties and taxes increased in the 1760s, Mainers tended to be disengaged politically, if only because the cost of sending delegates to the Massachusetts assembly was too great for most communities to bear. However, the effects of the Coercive Acts, especially the Crown's closing of the port of Boston in June 1774, were felt immediately throughout the district, and especially on the coast. The only cargo Maine merchants could send to Boston was firewood; but they were forced to return empty.

Revolution

MAINERS WERE by no means unified in their feelings towards the crown. Among those merchants who did not support the revolutionaries' aims, some felt restricted trade under British control to be better than no trade at all. Others looked for ways to take advantage of a bad situation. Still others recognized that some remote communities could not sustain themselves without the benefit of food and other goods brought by trade. Such was the case at Machias, where the family of Boston merchant Ichabod Jones had developed the area's lumber trade in the decade before the Revolution. As early as 1774, many of the colonies had decided to close their ports to ships from England in retaliation for the Coercive Acts. More attuned to the potential for profit than the uncertainties of rebellion, Jones continued to trade lumber to Boston, where the British authorities were desperate even for firewood, in exchange for food and other goods for Machias and its surrounding communities.

In acknowledgment of the difficulties Jones faced, Vice Admiral Samuel Graves ordered the armed sloop HMS *Margaretta*, 4 guns, to accompany Jones's sloops *Polly* and the inaptly named

Unity. The little convoy's reception was mixed, some of the 600 or so townsmen agreeing to trade with Jones, and others refusing. A rebel plot to seize Jones while he was at church failed, but in the confusion that followed, the majority of the town sided with the rebels. On June 3, 1775, Jeremiah O'Brien commandeered an armed sloop and sailed out in pursuit of the *Margaretta*, whose young commander had decided to quit the town. In the ensuing engagement, the British vessel was seized, as were two others that had sailed to the mouth of the Machias River.

When news of the action reached Boston, a furious Admiral Graves ordered Lieutenant Henry Mowat, HMS *Canceaux*, to punish the rebels, and not only in Machias.

MY DESIGN is to chastise Marblehead, Salem, Newbury Port, Cape Anne Harbor, Portsmouth, Ipswich, Saco, Falmouth in Casco Bay, and particularly Mechias where the

A line cut of the first naval engagement of the American Revolution, in which Jeremiah O'Brien, "The Machias Admiral," defeated the Royal Navy sloop *Margaretta*.
COURTESY MAINE HISTORICAL SOCIETY, PORTLAND

Margaretta was taken, the Officer commanding her killed, and the People made Prisoners, and where the *Diligent* Schooner was seized and the Officers and Crew carried Prisoners up the Country, and where preparations I am informed are now making to invade the Province of Nova Scotia.

This was an impressive list of potential targets, but in the end weather and other circumstances whittled it down to only one, Falmouth, whose location Mowat well knew. Shortly after the Battles of Lexington and Concord on April 19, 1775, a Loyalist merchant named Thomas Coulson wanted to unload a cargo of sails and rigging for a ship he was fitting out at Falmouth. In May, under threat from the local militia for refusing to observe the colonists' retaliatory embargo on British trade, he applied to the British commanders in Boston for protection, which came in the form of Mowat's *Canceaux*. Militiamen from the surrounding communities managed to seize Mowat on Falmouth Neck, an action that almost precipitated a battle between the citizens of Falmouth, who were exposed to the *Canceaux*'s guns, and rebels from inland towns who had little to fear from either warships or a ban on trade. Mowat was eventually released, and he left Falmouth accompanied by Loyalist exiles and with the sincere apologies of the town's leading citizens.

When Mowat returned on October 17 with a squadron of four ships to avenge the loss of the *Margaretta*, he allowed the inhabitants one night to evacuate the town after they offered to surrender their arms. In the meantime, country militiamen arrived bristling with defiance and Mowat had no recourse but to fire on Falmouth. By nightfall 400 buildings had been destroyed and the British had captured two ships and sunk eleven others. Worse still, many of the militiamen took advantage of the confusion to loot the property of merchants and others, an act that further aggravated relations between town and country.

While Mowat and the rebels were laying waste to Falmouth, one of the more remarkable expeditions of the war was making its way through Maine for an invasion of Quebec. In September Benedict Arnold had been dispatched from the Continental Army outside Boston to lead an army of a thousand men into Canada to rendezvous with a similar force being sent north from New York. The intent was to seize Quebec and rally French Canadians (who had been under British rule since 1763) to the rebel cause. Arnold's force sailed to Georgetown and proceeded up the Kennebec to Gardinerstown. There, the force transferred to a flotilla of about 200 bateaux, heavy, pine-on-oak planked boats of a kind used by loggers well into the twentieth century. For the route across the mountains of western Maine birchbark canoes—rugged but light and more easily carried across portages—would have been far more suitable.

If the choice of craft wasn't bad enough, the pine was unseasoned, and the boats could not withstand the rough treatment they received. One expedition survivor later wrote: "Could we then have come within reach of the villains who constructed these crazy things, they would fully have experienced the effects of our vengeance. Avarice or a desire to destroy us—perhaps both—must have been their motive." Passing Fort Western in modern Augusta, Skowhegan Falls, and the all-but-abandoned Abnaki village of Norridgewock, Arnold's troops soon turned west to begin the arduous overland trek via the Dead River, Chain of Lakes, and the Chaudière River for the descent to Quebec. Known today as the Arnold Trail, the route from the Atlantic to the St. Lawrence was originally pioneered by the Abnaki. By the time Arnold's bedraggled force arrived in early November, nearly a third of the men had died or deserted. Another hundred would die in the failed New Year's Eve assault, but the campaign convinced the British to maintain a costly presence in Canada. The most extensive use of Maine's rivers by any military campaign, Arnold's march illustrates an insurmountable limitation of Maine geography. Despite the number of navigable Maine rivers, none is navigable beyond the state's borders. By sea across the Gulf of Maine and around Cape

Breton to the St. Lawrence, Arnold's expedition might have taken less than a month, and with considerably less hardship.

Such an attempt would have been impossible in the face of the Royal Navy. The Gulf of Maine was also thick with privateers throughout the Revolution, and though Loyalist (and opportunist) raiders frequently preyed upon coastal settlements in Maine, Nova Scotia fared no better at the hands of rebel privateers. The British were particularly anxious about the activities of privateers operating out of Machias, from where rebellious colonists attempted to export the revolution to Nova Scotia. Just as there were Loyalists in the thirteen colonies, there were rebel sympathizers in British Canada. But in 1779 the Loyalists gained the upper hand in eastern Maine.

The previous year, a group of refugees in Halifax had fleshed out a plan for the creation of a new Loyalist province of New Ireland between the Penobscot and St. Croix Rivers. The government accepted the proposal and in June 1779, a force of five ships carrying 700 British soldiers sailed to Bagaduce (Pentagoët—now Castine) and erected a fort. Greatly alarmed by this sudden turn of events, which gave the British a port 200 miles closer to Boston than Halifax, the General Court of Massachusetts ordered the assembly of a large fleet to retake Bagaduce. Under the command of Brigadier General Solomon Lovell and Commodore Dudley Saltonstall, thirty-nine ships—three from the Continental navy, three from the Massachusetts state navy, thirteen privateers, and twenty privately owned transports—sailed from Boston with 1,500 soldiers, many of them forced to join the fleet by impressment.

The expedition's disastrous outcome was due not to the American soldiers, fearful and inexperienced though they were, but to a failure of leadership. Neither Saltonstall nor Lovell could capitalize on their troops' initial successes ashore. On August 13 the Americans were on the verge of capturing the fort when a British squadron of five ships was seen coming up Penobscot Bay with a following wind. Saltonstall's ships fled up the bay and,

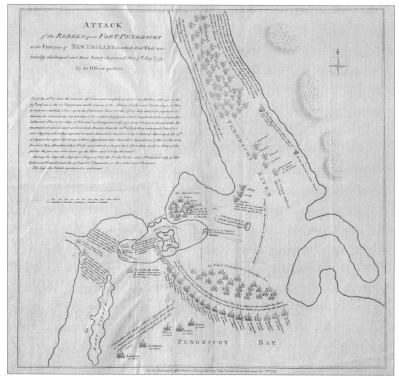

A plan of the "Attack of the Rebels upon Fort Penobscot...drawn
by an Officer present," from *Rapin's Impartial History of England*
(1785). For reasons unknown, the topography is reversed.
COURTESY OSHER MAP LIBRARY, UNIVERSITY OF SOUTHERN MAINE, PORTLAND

overtaken by the British before they could reach the Penobscot
River, the Americans burned or scuttled every ship that escaped
capture. The Penobscot expedition—the Americans' largest
naval operation of the Revolution—was the worst American
naval defeat until Japan's surprise attack on Pearl Harbor in
1941. Apart from Machias and the surrounding towns, the
British controlled eastern Maine until after the Revolution. Bagaduce became a haven for Loyalists—merchants especially, who
continued to trade for the duration of the war—while the Royal
Navy seized 80 or 90 percent of the vessels in Lincoln County.

One difficulty the United States faced was the lack of a proper
navy to protect its citizens' interests. The few ships that com-

prised the Continental navy were built only after the fighting began. To distribute work more evenly, these were constructed at yards throughout the colonies, including Kittery. The second ship launched for the navy at Langdon's Island was *Ranger*. The Continental Congress appointed John Paul Jones to command the 18-gun ship on June 14, 1777. By coincidence, Congress the same day passed the first flag act: "Resolved: that the flag of the thirteen United States be thirteen stripes, alternate red and white; that the union be thirteen stars, white in a blue field, representing a new constellation." With a crew drawn largely from Kittery and the surrounding area, *Ranger* sailed for France on November 1 and arrived a month later with two prizes to her credit. She also carried news of the American victory at the Battle of Saratoga, which convinced the French to formalize their alliance with the United States. On February 14, 1778, after the American ship had rendered honors to the French fleet in Quiberon Bay, Admiral LaMotte Piquet's flagship, *Robuste*, became the first foreign ship to salute the Stars and Stripes. Jones and *Ranger* then took the Revolution to the very shores of England, raiding the English port of Whitehaven, and then capturing HMS *Duke* (20 guns). *Ranger* subsequently returned to the United States and was captured at the fall of Charleston, South Carolina, in 1780. By the end of the war, the navy effectively had no ships and it was disbanded formally in 1785.

Independence and Dependence

As IT HAD the fledgling navy, the seven-year Revolution devastated much of the United States. Government finances were a shambles and the economy, so dependent on trade, was in ruins. For the first time, American merchants were on their own in the world marketplace. Gone were the Navigation Acts that restricted what merchants could import and export from American ports. But with them went the guarantees of employment for English seamen in English ships, and the protection of the Royal Navy. American ships were now barred from ports in the British Isles, Canada, India, Ceylon and minor Asian islands, British colonies on the Gold Coast of Africa, Bermuda, the Bahamas, Jamaica, the Leeward and Windward Islands, Antigua and Barbados in the West Indies, and Belize in Central America. In England, many agreed with the sentiments of one lord who argued that in its trade policies Parliament should "endeavor to divert the whole Anglo-American trade to British bottoms." There was little money to replace the domestic merchant fleets destroyed or captured during the war and although American harbors were busy again, they were crowded with foreign ships. The postwar depression was not permanent, however, and conditions improved markedly following the ratification of the Constitution and the federal government's subsequent intervention on behalf of American merchants.

One of President George Washington's first initiatives was the creation of the Treasury Department to raise money for the government. This it did partly by imposing customs duties on imported goods. Duties on goods carried in American ships were lower than those for goods in foreign bottoms, but any duties cut into profits. Smuggling—a problem since before the Revolution—was again widespread. To counter this, Treasury Secretary Alexander Hamilton established the U.S. Revenue Cutter Service (a forerunner of the modern Coast Guard), whose missions were to catch smugglers, protect the merchant marine, and defend coastal waters. Well aware that the Royal Navy's heavy-handed enforcement of similar tax laws had been a primary cause of the Revolution, Hamilton enjoined his officers to keep in mind "that their countrymen are freemen, and, as such, are impatient of everything that bears the least mark of a domineering spirit."

The first officer appointed to the service—and the first maritime officer of any kind appointed under the Constitution—Captain Hopley Yeaton exemplified this high standard throughout his career with the Revenue Service. A veteran of the Kittery-built *Raleigh* during the Revolution, he assumed command of the cutter *Scammel* on patrols between the Piscataqua and the Canadian border. He later retired to Lubec, on the shores of Passamaquoddy Bay, but in 1803 he was given a new commission, which he held until the end of 1809. He died three years later, at the age of seventy. So distinguished was Yeaton's career that in 1979 the remains of this founding father of the Coast Guard were transferred to the U.S. Coast Guard Academy Chapel in New London, Connecticut.

Lighthouses are no guarantee of safety. The bark *Annie C. Maguire* wrecked in the shadow of Portland Head Light on Christmas Eve 1886, ninety-six years after the lighthouse was commissioned. The crew made it safely to land, but the ship was a total loss.
COURTESY PORTLAND HARBOR MUSEUM, SOUTH PORTLAND

Hand-in-hand with raising revenue and eradicating smuggling, the Treasury Department also assumed responsibility for "the necessary support, maintenance, and repairs of all lighthouses" and other aids to navigation around the country. This was the ninth piece of legislation enacted by Congress, and its first dedicated to public works. The Treasury's priority was the completion of Portland Head Light on Cape Elizabeth, which the state of Massachusetts had started three years before, and it began operation in 1790. The decision to build a lighthouse at Portland testifies to the quality of the port's location and potential. By some accounts, as late as 1787 there was "not a ship owned in town." Seven years later there were eighty.

Such growth was not peculiar to Portland, and ports to the south and east were sending ships coastwise, to the West Indies and overseas. The eastward movement of people and commerce already evident in the pre-war decades was made manifest by the

Treasury Department's creation of three Customs Districts for Maine, at Portland/Falmouth, Bath, and Wiscasset. (After the Revolution Wiscasset became the political seat of Lincoln County, replacing the more inaccessible Pownalborough 10 miles up the Sheepscot River.) New districts were created and combined throughout the nineteenth century, and in 1859 there were a total of thirteen in Maine. Bureaucratic streamlining led to the creation of a single customs district comprising all of Maine and New Hampshire in 1913.

In addition to supporting American commerce with favorable duties, Congress helped stimulate trade and shipbuilding by paying a "bounty" to cod fishermen. When negotiating the treaty that ended the War of Independence, John Adams had been adamant in protecting American fishermen's "Right to take Fish" on the Grand Banks and elsewhere, and about preserving their "freedom" to dry their catch on the shores of Newfoundland and Labrador. A Massachusetts native, Adams knew well the economic importance of cod to that Commonwealth (of which Maine was still a province), whose General Court in 1784 passed a motion:

> THAT LEAVE might be given to hang up the representation of a Codfish in the room where the House sit, as a memorial of the importance of the Cod-fishery to the welfare of this Commonwealth, as had been usual formerly.

By the end of the war, virtually all of the sixty Maine vessels engaged in the offshore fisheries had been lost. The federal codfish bounty began in 1789 as a guaranteed payment for fish caught for export; in a sense, the bounty merely compensated for the tariffs imposed on imported salt and other commodities essential to the industry. However, to further protect American fishermen, hefty duties were imposed on imported fish. Three years later, the government began to pay a per-ton rate for boats engaged in fishing at least four months of the year. Before 1819 the maximum bounty for vessels under 30 tons was $2.60 per ton, and $4.00 per ton for vessels over 30 tons. Under this system, the "codfish aristocracy" of Massachusetts proper received a disproportionate share of the bounty because they generally built bigger boats than their counterparts in Maine. Overall, the fishing industry certainly benefited from the first round of bounties: between 1790 and 1810, total fishing-boat tonnage more than tripled, from 20,000 to 69,000 tons. Yet in the decade after 1796, Maine fishing tonnage grew barely 60 percent, from 6,100 to 9,800 tons. After the lower rate increased to $3.50 per ton in 1819, Maine fishermen owned about 20 percent of all codfishing vessels over twenty tons (about forty feet long), double their share of the fleet before then.

American commerce received another boost in 1793, the start of a twenty-two-year period of almost uninterrupted warfare between Britain and France. The Royal Navy quickly closed the major trade routes to French ships and those of her allies. Preaching the doctrine that "free ships make free goods"—that is, if a merchant's country wasn't at war, he could ship goods to either of the belligerents without being seized by the other—the United States quickly became the world's largest neutral shipper. Merchants thrived especially on routes between the French and Spanish Caribbean colonies and Europe. In 1794 Jay's Treaty opened more of the British West Indies to American ships. The combined effects of these beneficial changes in fortune were staggering. American exports doubled between 1790 and 1807, and re-exports rose from $300,000 to $59 million, and Maine merchants certainly shared in the general prosperity. In the mid-1790s, a French visitor traveling south from Portland confided to his diary:

> THE NEARER you approach Boston, so much the more does the whole country appear to assume an air of business and industry. Not a creek but ships are building in it; not a river's mouth so small, but merchants' companies are there

in possession of ships; no situation where a mill could stand, on which there has not been a mill erected. Falmouth [Portland], Pepperellborough, Saco, Biddeford, Kennebunk, Berwick, carry on a trade far superior to that at the small towns through which I had passed on my way hither.

A downside to Jay's Treaty was that it barred French privateers from using U.S. ports, and in retaliation the French government authorized its corsairs to prey on American ships, hundreds of which were snapped up in short order. Relations with France deteriorated so quickly that Congress established the Department of the Navy and authorized the construction of six naval shipyards—the first located on Seavey Island in Kittery—and the completion of six frigates originally ordered to combat Barbary corsairs. The Quasi War involved a good deal of diplomatic intrigue which spilled over into domestic politics, but fighting per se was limited to engagements between naval frigates and corsairs in the Caribbean. In the long run, the Barbary corsairs proved a far greater threat to American commerce and identity.

So long as colonial merchants sailed under the protection of the British flag, these had been little threat, but following independence, American merchants were subject to capture and enslavement for ransom unless the government offered protection money. Euphemistically known as tribute, this took the form of masts, other naval stores, and entire ships such as the 36-gun frigate *Crescent*, built at a private yard in Kittery. The government authorized construction of six frigates to combat the corsairs early in the 1790s, but halted work when a truce was reached with Algiers. No sooner had the so-called Quasi War with France wound down than Barbary corsairs resumed their pursuit of American ships. By now the country had a fleet, and in retaliation the U.S. Navy established a blockade of North African ports. In 1801 the pasha of Tripoli declared war. One of the young navy's most able and effective commanders was Commodore Edward Preble whose leadership was so marked that his junior officers, many of whom would serve in the War of 1812, came to be known as Preble's Boys.

Born in Falmouth (Portland), Preble fought in each of America's first three naval conflicts. He served in the Massachusetts state navy during the Revolution, was held in the prison ship *Jersey* at New York, and after his release led the cutting out of a British brig at Castine under heavy fire from shore. When peace came, Preble spent fifteen years as a merchant captain sailing out of Boston. He further distinguished himself in command of the revenue cutter *Pickering* at the start of the Quasi War, and in 1799 was made captain of the USS *Essex* on the Navy's first assignment in the East Indies. He acquired a reputation as a harsh disciplinarian, generous with the lash, but his mission was successful, and he escorted home a dozen merchantmen laden with valuable cargoes of spices and coffee.

Flagship of Commodore Edward Preble's Mediterranean squadron during the Barbary War, the USS *Constitution* visited Portland in the 1930s. She is being towed past Ram Island Ledge Light (1905), but otherwise the scene would be familiar to any Portlander of Preble's day. COURTESY HERB ADAMS

Sailing in USS *Constitution*, Preble commanded the U.S. squadron in the Mediterranean for fourteen months in 1803–04, during which he bombarded the port of Tripoli. Relieved of command before the end of the war, he retired to Portland where he became a shipbuilder, though he continued to advise the Navy. In an 1806 letter to the Secretary of the Navy he gave his blessing to the site of the shipyard on Seavey Island declaring it to have "more natural advantage than any other place I have met with for a Navy Yard." Prone to ulcers, the dyspeptic Commodore died in August 1807 at the age of forty-six.

With the close of the Barbary Wars, American commerce in the Mediterranean was safe from North African corsairs, and merchants were riding high on the proceeds from an international trade that already spanned the globe. So busy was the port of Portland that several months before Preble's death, retired shipmaster Lemuel Moody took it upon himself to arrange for the construction of an 82-foot-high octagonal observatory on Munjoy Hill, at the eastern end of the Portland peninsula. With the aid of a high-powered telescope, observers would be able to see incoming ships as they neared the port, and with a system of flags, to signal their approach to agents and owners along the Fore River a mile away. Observers would also be able to report on any ships in distress.

Although American trade was very profitable, Britain and France posed a far greater risk to merchants than the corsairs ever could. Now embroiled in the Napoleonic Wars, the two belligerents declared each other's ports under blockade, tightening the noose around international trade with a series of decrees (French) and Orders in Council (British) between 1804 and 1806. Despite American insistence that United States merchants had the right to trade what and where they wanted, their ships were now subject to arrest on the high seas, their goods to confiscation, and their sailors to involuntary service, at least in the Royal Navy. To counter this, in December President Thomas Jefferson urged Congress to pass the Embargo Act closing American ports to foreign trade. His rationale was that once Britain and France realized how dependent they were upon American shipping, they would change course.

Signed into law in December 1807, Jefferson's Embargo Act was a disaster. In a single year the volume of foreign goods entering America was cut in half, and although the Embargo lasted only fourteen months, foreign tonnage would not exceed 1 million tons again until 1816. Nationwide, an estimated 55,000 jobs in maritime trades were lost, and in some Maine towns, unemployment reached 60 percent. Import duties received in Portland plummeted, from $342,909 in 1806 to $37,633 in 1808.

Hardship was as swift and widespread as it was severe. On January 29, 1808—only five weeks after the start of the Embargo—the Reverend Edward Payson of Portland wrote his father:

Signals at Port Land Observatory, attributed to Lemuel Moody, shows his Observatory and the flags of merchants registered at the Observatory.
COURTESY MAINE HISTORICAL SOCIETY, PORTLAND

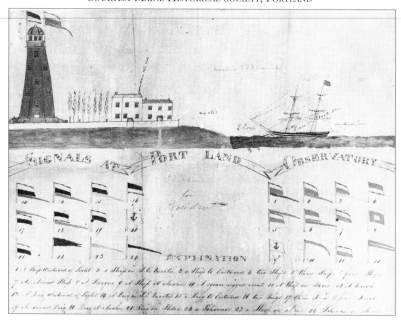

A LARGE number of the most wealthy merchants have already failed, and numbers more are daily following, so that we are threatened with universal bankruptcy. Two failures alone have thrown at least three hundred persons, besides sailors, out of employ.... The poorhouse is already full.... All confidence is lost; no man will trust his neighbor.... I cannot describe...the distress we are in.

In Bath, sixteen ships and twenty-seven brigs were tied up for the duration of the Embargo, in addition to a number of sloops and schooners. Many prosperous merchants were wiped out. One of those who weathered the storm was William King, who later recalled that he had five ships and three brigs "loaded for foreign voyages" (and another brig "not loaded") tied up in the Kennebec during the crisis. A political ally of President Jefferson who also served as Maine's first governor, King wrote in 1825, "...no one ever heard any complaint from me, although the actual loss, at the most modest calculations of charter, was $5,558 per month...exclusive of interest on money on the amount of the cargoes from Dec. 22, 1807, to May 1809." The year before the Embargo, Wiscasset had sixty-seven merchant ships at sea in foreign trade. In 1808 two ships were in trade while another thirty swung at anchor.

Not all merchants had the wherewithal to sit out the Embargo or were content to go bankrupt, and although the Embargo was rigidly enforced, there were some successful evasions. The ship *Sally* ran out of the Kennebec bound for London with lumber, only to be shot at as she ran past the battery at Fort Popham. (This fort was built in 1775; the Fort Popham visible today dates from the Civil War.) The gunners aimed high, as they would on other occasions, and the *Sally* proceeded to England. On another occasion the 52-ton sloop *Adoniram* was loaded with an illicit cargo of flour and about 22,000 pounds of fish brought out by the boatload as she lay off Monhegan Island. Her master sailed her for Demerara, Guayana, and, "We accordingly arrived at that port and sold both vessel and cargo for cash, and after remaining there thirty days, I received the pay in British and other gold."

Vessels in coastal trade were required to post a bond that they would only land their cargoes in United States ports. According to American merchants, the Embargo coincided with a period of abnormally bad weather—probably the worst weather ever on the East Coast. Captains sailing on coastal passages mysteriously found themselves blown off course and forced to run for harbors of refuge, all of which happened to be foreign ports. But of course it is an ill wind that blows no one good, and the masters could at least console themselves that the sale of their cargoes in these forbidden ports fetched a much higher price than they would have at home. And if they didn't sell their ship, too, they could engage in a profitable trade that kept them out of United States ports for the duration of the Embargo.

One port that did uncommonly well during the Embargo was Eastport. Located on Moose Island in Passamaquoddy Bay, Eastport is the easternmost city in the lower forty-eight States. At the time of the Embargo, the population numbered less than 1,000 people, and whether the island was part of the United States or British Canada wasn't settled finally until 1808. Because of its easy access to foreign ports across the bay, and the New Brunswick government's temporary suspension of the ban on importing enumerated goods like food and naval stores, Eastport quickly became a smugglers' haven. It is estimated that at least 160,000 barrels of flour were shipped to Eastport in 1808 to be carried across the border at rates of between twelve cents and three dollars per barrel. The government attempted to eradicate this illicit trade and at one time or another the waters around Eastport were patrolled by four gunboats, the frigates USS *Wasp* and USS *Chesapeake* (the latter under Stephen Decatur, one of Preble's Boys), and Revenue Service cutters under the likes of such men as Hopley Yeaton.

Repeal of the Embargo Act marked a turn for the better, but there were still restrictions on trade with Britain and France.

Worse yet, the Madison administration was agitating for war against Great Britain. Although the primary motive for war was a desire for territorial expansion in the west at Canada's expense, the rallying cry was "Free trade and sailors' rights"—the latter a reference to the Royal Navy's unlawful "impressment" of English sailors it found serving in American ships. New England merchants wanted nothing to do with a war that would disturb their business, and they were particularly incensed when Congress declared war on behalf of the U.S. merchant marine without voting an increase in naval spending.

With opportunities for normal commerce denied them during the War of 1812, Maine mariners flocked to privateers with which to disrupt British shipping. Some of these cruised in European waters, but there were plenty of prizes in the Gulf of Maine, and ships such as Freeport's *Dash* (fifteen prizes before she disappeared on Georges Bank), the Wiscasset-built *Grand*

The bloody battle between HMS *Boxer* and USS *Enterprise*, off Monhegan Island, ended in the deaths of both commanding officers, who are buried in Portland overlooking Casco Bay.
COURTESY MAINE HISTORICAL SOCIETY, PORTLAND.

Turk (sold to Salem interests, for whom she captured thirty prizes), and the Portland-built "million-dollar privateer" *Fox* achieved a well-deserved renown. The only naval engagement in Maine waters was fought near Portland between HMS *Boxer* and USS *Enterprise* (both 14 guns) on September 5, 1813. Strategically insignificant, the engagement cost the lives of both commanders, who are buried in a cemetery on Portland's Eastern Promenade. Following Napoleon's abdication in April 1814, the British had more men and materiel to spare for their American campaign, and they declared a blockade of the East Coast.

Prior to the declaration of the blockade, there was a determined effort in the eastern part of the state to limit the consequences of the war to the extent possible. The citizens of Eastport and the neighboring Passamaquoddy Bay town of St. Andrews, on the Canadian side, refrained from harassing each other's trade. Rather than sweep American fishermen from the sea, as they might have done easily, the Royal Navy confined them to a restricted area. Merchants on both sides fell victim to privateers sailing under both flags, but it was a point of honor for Eastport that none of her citizens owned a privateer. As it had during Jefferson's Embargo, smuggling prospered in Eastport until the summer of 1814. On July 11 a squadron of fifteen Royal Navy ships captured Eastport. Machias fell in August, followed by Castine and Bangor in September. Thereafter, Eastport could engage in legal trade with St. John, Halifax, and Castine, and the illicit trade moved offshore, to Indian and Campobello Islands. The territory east of the Penobscot remained in British hands until 1818. Far from suffering under a repressive yoke, Eastport emerged from this period of British rule with strong connections to international markets and as ready to take part in the postwar prosperity as anywhere else in Maine.

The Navy Yard on Seavey Island in the Piscataqua River. The
bridges lead to Kittery; in the distance is Portsmouth, New
Hampshire, from which the shipyard takes its name.
COURTESY BRICK STORE MUSEUM, KENNEBUNK

Why a Maine Shipyard Is
Named for a New Hampshire City

Its name and New Hampshire's occasional pretensions to ownership
notwithstanding, the Portsmouth Naval Shipyard is located on Seavey Island in Kittery, Maine. According to one explanation of the
name, when the Navy Department in Washington, DC, sent mail to
the shipyard in Kittery, Maine, they addressed it through the post
office in neighboring Portsmouth, south across the Piscataqua River.
The U.S. Post Office follows the same logic today: the Maine cities
of Kittery, Eliot, and York all have ZIP codes starting with 03, the
marker for New Hampshire, as opposed to Maine's 04 designation.
Portsmouth Naval Shipyard phone numbers all have Maine's "207"
area code, and the facility is accessible by bridge only from the Maine
side of the Piscataqua River.

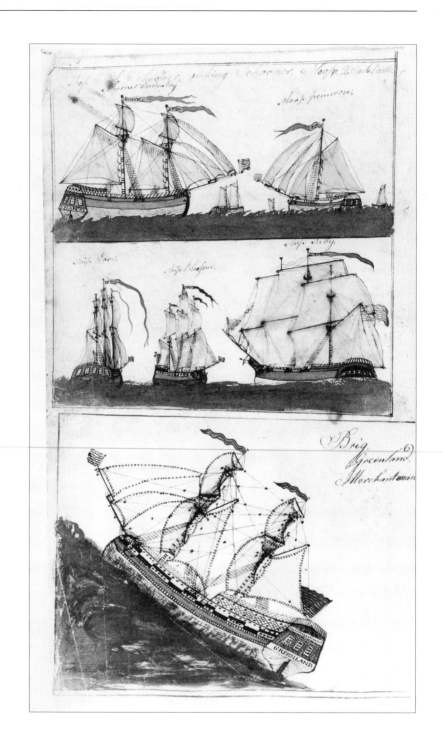

A Century of Ships

IN THE PERIOD before the War
of 1812, Maine as a whole had established the basis for a com-
merce-based prosperity that would last well past mid-century.
Soon after the war, Maine seceded from Massachusetts and was
admitted to the Union as a state in its own right in 1820. The
new state seal and the choice of the capital symbolize the spirit
of the age. The seal depicts a farmer and a sailor standing on
either side of a pine tree under the Latin motto, *Dirigo*—"I
lead." Lumber and seafaring were, of course, the state's two most
important trades, but it would be several decades before agricultural output expanded significantly beyond the subsistence level.
Transferring the capital from Portland to Augusta (in 1832) reflected the fact that the center of population was moving north
and east away from the state's colonial origins in York and Cumberland Counties. But though it is 45 miles from the ocean, Au-

Opposite: "Top Sail Schooner, Fishing Schooner, Sloop. 2 Sail
Boats. Schooner *Industry*, Sloop *Primrose*, Ship *Dove*, Ship *Blossom*,
Ship *Sally*, Brig *Greenland*." From the Ammi Quint account book
(1803–33). COURTESY MAINE HISTORICAL SOCIETY, PORTLAND

gusta is also the head of navigation on the Kennebec River, and the average range of tide there is more than four feet. However developed the interior would become, the state still depended on access to the sea for its livelihood.

Saltwater commerce remained the most important factor in Maine's development through the Civil War. Several kinds of vessels were involved. The deepwater trader with the oldest pedigree is the full-rigged ship and its forerunners. In the seventeenth century, this was a three-masted vessel setting square sails on the fore and main masts, and a triangular lateen sail on the mizzen. A square spritsail was also set beneath the bowsprit. Bartholomew Gosnold's *Concord*, which visited the coast in 1602, was 55 tons (about 39 feet on the keel) and sailed with a crew of 32 men. The Pilgrims' *Mayflower* of 1622 was 180 tons (about 100 feet) and carried about 125 passengers and crew all told. Over the next 200 years, the lateen mizzen sail gave way to a four-sided gaff mizzen sail called a spanker. Fore-and-aft triangular sails called staysails were set between the foremast and jibboom, or between the masts. The nineteenth century saw further refinements to this rig, including the addition of sails to taller masts, and the splitting of larger topsails and topgallant sails into upper and lower to make them easier to handle.* If square sails were also set on the mizzenmast, the rig was a full-rigged ship; if not, the vessel was known as a bark.

Square-rigged vessels tended to remain fairly small—no more than about 300 tons—and slow through the early years of the nineteenth century. A development of the late seventeenth and early eighteenth century, the two-masted, square-rigged brigantine (sometimes abbreviated to brig) became the workhorse of New England's long-distance trade.** In the colonial period,

---

* From the deck up, the sails on a mainmast of a typical full-rigged ship of the 1800s were: course, topsail, topgallant, royal, and, by the 1830s, skysail. Topsails were split into upper and lower in the 1850s, and topgallants in the 1880s.

** Originally brigantine and brig referred to the same rig. By current usage, a brig is a two-masted vessel square-rigged on both masts, and a brigantine is square-rigged on the foremast and fore-and-aft-rigged on the main mast.

they were sailed in both transatlantic and West Indies trade. They tended to have greater carrying capacity for a given length than schooners, and they were less expensive to build and man than ships. In the first few years after the Revolution, Bath shipbuilders launched no ships at all and contented themselves with brigs about 75 feet long and 160 or 170 tons. Schooners, which had even leaner manning requirements, in the same period tended to be about 65 to 70 feet long and about 90 to 115 tons. Brigs continued to grow in size, and after the War of 1812 they were dominant in the West Indies trade. Passages from northern Caribbean ports like Havana and St. Thomas took about 18 days, and 34 days from ports such as Demerara, Guyana, on the South American mainland. In time, the full-rigged ship superceded the brig, and on coastwise routes the schooner (sometimes fitted with a square topsail on the foremast) replaced the brigantine.

With the close of the Napoleonic Wars and the coming of the Pax Britannica—a period of peaceful international trade guaranteed by an omnipotent and no longer hostile Royal Navy—ships began to increase in size and speed. This was due both to advances in ship design and an improved understanding of hydrodynamics (the study of how things move through the water) as well as more favorable economic conditions. Between 1825 and 1859, a total of 90 full-rigged ships were built at Kennebunkport—19 by 1844 and 71 between 1845 and 1859. (The increased reliance on ships came largely at the expense of brigs. Between 1815 and 1850, for instance, Bath launched 116 brigs, only 9 of them in the last decade.) In this thirty-year period, however, the average size of Kennebunkport ships more than tripled, from 300 to 905 tons. Full-rigged ships were of course not the only type of craft launched at Kennebunkport, where six yards turned out a total of 638 ships, brigs, schooners, barks, sloops, and even a few steam vessels in the eight decades before 1880. In so doing, the builders had to overcome a number of natural obstacles, the most significant being a series of shallow falls between the builders' yards and the open ocean. In 1849 a lock

The 916-ton ship *Arno* being floated down the Kennebunk
towards the lock in 1857. The vessel is buoyed by scows forward
and floats astern so that she draws as little water as possible, and
mast sections are secured alongside. DRAWING BY SAM MANNING,
COURTESY BRICK STORE MUSEUM, KENNEBUNK

gate was built that enabled pilots conning the ships downriver to
increase the volume of water above the falls so that larger ships
could clear the shallows on their way to the sea.

One of the trades in which Maine shippers excelled was the
cotton trade. New England still did not have many export goods
with ready markets in Europe, but British and other mills had an
insatiable appetite for southern cotton. So a new three-legged
trade system arose. New England ships freighted lumber and
other raw materials to southern ports—chiefly Charleston, Savannah, Mobile, and New Orleans. There, they loaded cotton
for Liverpool and Le Havre, where they would load finished
goods for the American market. There was also a coastwise trade
in which cotton was carried to New York to be loaded aboard

larger packet ships. The packet trade was an American innovation in which shippers fixed the dates on which their ships would sail to Great Britain rather than wait until the ship had a full cargo, as was the customary practice.

The apogee of American square-rigger building had two distinct phases on either side of the Civil War. Long years of illicit smuggling, privateering, and slave trading (both before and after the latter was outlawed), combined with experience gained in the cotton trade and building packets for faster and more reliable service, led to the development of ever-faster hull designs and rigs. The culmination of what one historian called "the search for speed under sail" was the development of the clipper ship. Extremely fast full-rigged ships of limited capacity and requiring large crews, clippers have a reputation that tends to exaggerate their commercial importance. But they excited their contemporaries in the same way that the supersonic Concorde fires our imagination today. They were prestige vessels, and so long as people were willing to pay inflated prices for the additional speed their owners and hard-driving captains promised (but could not always deliver), they flourished.

The clipper form began to blossom in the China trades, where the extra costs associated with speed were offset by the high value of the cargoes—tea and silk—and the fact that unduly long voyages were expensive because investors' money was tied up longer. The same factors were at play to an even greater degree in the California gold rush of 1849 and the Australian gold rush of 1851. As long-distance trade grew, shipbuilders began to incorporate innovations suggested by experience or dictated by necessity. In the cotton trade, for instance, as ships increased in size, the shallow draft at the mouth of the Mississippi River forced designers to build ships with flatter bottoms. Contrary to expectation, the hull form made for some fast ships.

Although comparatively few clippers were built in Maine—most came from New York and Boston yards—a number of exceptional ships slid down the ways in the 1850s. Named for

Jenny Lind, the famous singer who made her American debut under the auspices of showman P. T. Barnum in 1850, *Nightingale* (1,066 tons, 185 feet) was adorned with two likenesses of "the Swedish Nightingale"—a bust figurehead on the bow and a stern carving showing her in a reclining position with a nightingale perched on her fingers. Before her launch at South Eliot on the Piscataqua in 1851, the ship advertised for passengers for a "Grand Trans-Atlantic Excursion to the World's Fair" in England. All told she was designed to carry 250 passengers, many of them in high style. The Boston firm of Sampson and Tappan purchased her for $75,000, but far from conveying New England gentry to the Crystal Palace Exhibition in London, on October 17 *Nightingale* cleared Boston for Melbourne in one of the first voyages to transport miners to the newly discovered Australian gold fields. Sailing on to Canton and Shanghai, she entered the lucrative tea trade and made four voyages to London, once with a stop in Melbourne and, in 1859, sailing to China via New York, Cape Horn, and San Francisco.

In 1860 she appears to have been used as a slaver between West Africa and the Caribbean, although her exact movements are unknown. The following year, the USS *Saratoga* seized *Nightingale* off Angola with 971 slaves aboard. The U.S. Navy used the ship as a supply depot and storeship during the Civil War, after which she was sold to the Western Union Company to work with a fleet of ships laying submarine cables across the Bering Strait. Sold back into merchant service, she passed through a succession of owners and spent her last seventeen years under Norwegian ownership freighting lumber from Quebec to Europe. She foundered at sea in 1893, but not before her crew were rescued by a passing vessel.

Another well-known Maine clipper was *Red Jacket* (2,355 tons, 251 feet), built by George Thomas in Rockland in 1853. Despite her great size—most clippers were under 2,000 tons— she was famous for her fine lines and graceful, lofty rig. Originally intended for work on the California run, on her maiden voyage she sailed from New York to Liverpool and set a transatlantic sailing ship record of 13 days, 1 hour, and 25 minutes dock-to-dock, a record that still stands almost 150 years later. Rather than enter the Cape Horn run to California, *Red Jacket* was chartered and eventually purchased by a British company to carry British immigrants out to Australia. In her heyday she was considered among the very best ships in the British merchant marine. Her subsequent career included voyages to India, and a return to the transatlantic run as a lumber carrier on the route between Quebec and Newcastle. After three decades in service, she was hulked in the Cape Verde Islands.

One of the only American clipper ships of which significant remains still exist, *Snow Squall* (742 tons, 157 feet) was built by Cornelius Butler on the Fore River in Cape Elizabeth (now South Portland) in 1851. Purchased after her maiden voyage to New York, she flew the house flag of Charles R. Green for thirteen years, carrying general cargo from New York (and twice from Boston) to the Orient, and returning with teas and silks. Three of her outward voyages were made via Cape Horn, the remainder of them via the Cape of Good Hope, often with stops in Australian ports. An extreme clipper, she was described at her launch as "very sharp at the bows, with a lean but handsomely graduated run, but from her great breadth of beam, will be enabled to carry well, while at the same time she cannot fail of being a fast sailor." And indeed she made some excellent runs, posting near-record times between ports on all oceans.

Nowhere was her speed put to better use than on a 94-day run between Penang and New York in 1863 under Captain James S. Dillingham, Jr. Near the Cape of Good Hope on July 28, 1863, the crew spoke the bark-rigged CSS *Tuscaloosa*, which neared *Snow Squall* under the American flag. When alongside, the Confederate raider showed her true colors and opened fire with her stern gun. Nothing daunted, Dillingham hauled close to the wind and *Snow Squall* showed her heels until *Tuscaloosa* gave up the chase four hours later. On her next voyage, *Snow Squall* sailed from New York for San Francisco, but on February 24, 1864, she was becalmed in the Strait of Le Maire east of Cape Horn and she drifted ashore on Tierra del Fuego. Leaking badly, *Snow Squall* put back to Stanley, Falkland Islands, where she was condemned. Dillingham made his way to Rio de Janeiro from where he sailed home in *Mondamin*, only to see that ship captured and burned by the Confederate raider CSS *Florida*.

Meanwhile, *Snow Squall* was incorporated into a makeshift jetty and over the next 122 years her hull was loaded with ballast stone, punctured for pilings, and subjected to the harsh elements of the South Atlantic. In the early 1980s, the *Snow Squall* Project was launched to save what remained of the Yankee clipper. The first of five visits took place just two weeks before Argentina invaded the British colony. Four years later, a section of the bow was cut free and returned to Maine. The bulk of this is now at the Maine Maritime Museum in Bath, and some pieces can be found at other museums such as the Portland Harbor Museum in South Portland, near where the clipper was built.

In many respects the clipper age was the climax of the American merchant marine. A number of factors conspired America's share in the carriage of world trade, with pronounced implications for Maine. In 1849, the year of the California gold rush, Great Britain repealed the last of its dreaded Navigation Acts. Ports once closed to American shipping were now open, and thanks to a reciprocal arrangement, American ports were now open to British ships. At the same time, the cost of American ships was rising, especially compared with the costs of shipbuilding in Canada. The surge in shipbuilding fueled by the California gold rush gradually subsided, and with the opening of the American West, Americans began to reorient themselves away from the sea. The first half of the nineteenth century had been a period of explosive growth for Maine. The population nearly quadrupled between 1800 and 1850, and the growth rate was faster than the national average until 1830. In the half century between 1845 and 1896, nineteen states joined the Union, all but two of them west of the Mississippi, and the area of the United States nearly tripled. The attraction of the American heartland, coupled with the completion of the transcontinental railroad in 1863, proved irresistible. In the decade after the Civil War, Maine's population actually declined, and between 1850 and 2000 it grew less than threefold.

Another factor was the Civil War itself. Unable to field a fleet capable of challenging the U.S. Navy on anything like equal terms, the Confederacy resorted to a number of expedient measures, making extensive use of ironclads, pioneering the use of submarine vessels, and relying heavily on armed raiders to sink as many American-flag ships as possible to force the collapse of the United States merchant marine. While inconclusive with respect to the Confederacy's immediate war aims, the policy had a devastating effect on America's deep-sea fleet especially: insurance rates rose 900 percent, and more than 900 ships were transferred to foreign registry. The commerce raiders did not limit themselves to merchant ships on the high seas, and one of their most daring raids brought the Civil War right into Casco Bay.

Among the more successful Confederate commerce raiders was the CSS *Florida*, the same ship that captured Captain Dillingham while homeward bound from the Falkland Islands after the loss of *Snow Squall*. Around the same time that the Maine clipper was fleeing from *Tuscaloosa* off South Africa in July of 1863, crew from *Florida* were setting in train a series of events that would lead to the capture of the U.S. Revenue Cutter *Caleb Cushing* in Casco Bay. The event had been set in motion in May, when *Florida* seized the merchant brig *Clarence* and fitted her out as a commerce raider under Lieutenant Charles W. Read. The *Clarence* went on to capture six more ships until Read decided to transfer his crew to the bark *Tacony*. Over the next twelve days *Tacony* captured fifteen vessels, most of them fishing schooners. On June 24 Read again transferred his crew to the fishing schooner *Archer*. On the evening of the 26th, the Southport schooner sailed into Portland Harbor, Read's intent being to capture the propeller steamship *Chesapeake* or to burn ships under construction or lying at the city's wharves. These ideas proved impractical so he decided instead to seize the *Caleb Cushing*. Cutting out the schooner was accomplished with relative ease, but by next morning the passenger steamers *Forest City* (a sidewheeler) and *Chesapeake* (a screw ship) were in hot pursuit. At about two o'clock in the afternoon, Read ordered the *Cushing* abandoned and blown up. *Archer* was caught later that day. Apart from the scare it gave coastal communities, the *Cushing* affair was of no lasting consequence.

There is an interesting coda to the *Caleb Cushing* affair. The revenue cutter's namesake was one of the foremost American diplomats of the nineteenth century. Following the Civil War, the United States insisted that Britain be held liable for the destruction wrought by British-built commerce raiders such as the *Florida* and the *Alabama*. The resulting proceedings came to be known as the *Alabama* claims, because that ship alone accounted for an estimated $5 million in direct losses before she was sunk in a duel with the Kittery-built screw sloop, USS *Kearsarge*, on June 19, 1864. Led by Cushing, the American delegation persuaded the international tribunal that Britain had not exercised "due diligence." Under the Treaty of Washington (1871), Britain was forced to pay the United States $15.5 million in damages.

The end of the Civil War found the American merchant marine in tatters. The hundreds of ships put in foreign registry to avoid capture by Confederate raiders could not return to the American flag even if they were owned in whole or part by Americans. This was due in large part to lobbying efforts by American shipbuilders who saw a great opportunity for themselves. The economic realities of the time were not in their favor. Overall, labor costs for wooden ships were higher than in Canada, and there was comparatively little iron shipbuilding in the United States at the time. There were also high tariffs on imported copper, iron, hemp, canvas, and other goods vital to the shipbuilding industry. Designed to foster native industry, these tariffs inhibited the development of the iron shipbuilding industry.

Maine could still build wooden ships economically because it had lower labor costs than were found elsewhere on the East Coast. Extensive though they were, Maine's forests were not inexhaustible and as early as the 1840s, Maine shipbuilders were using a variety of woods imported from southern states and elsewhere, as they do today. Henry Wadsworth Longfellow's 1849 narrative poem, "The Building of the Ship" is best known for its triumphant closing lines, "Thou, too, sail on, O Ship of State!" which reportedly moved Abraham Lincoln to tears. Yet the Portland-born, Bowdoin-educated poet was familiar with the shipwright's work, and for all its allegorical meaning, the poem contains several references to actual shipbuilding practice, including the importation of wood:

Covering many a rood of ground,
Lay the timber piled around;
Timber of chestnut, and elm, and oak,
And scattered here and there, with these,
The knarred and crooked cedar knees;
Brought from regions far away,
From Pascagoula's sunny bay,
And the banks of the roaring Roanoke!
Ah! what a wondrous thing it is
To note how many wheels of toil
One thought, one word, can set in motion!
There's not a ship that sails the ocean,
But every climate, every soil,
Must bring its tribute, great or small,
And help to build the wooden wall!

Among the first builders to import wood to Maine was Edward O'Brien of Thomaston, one of the pre-eminent shipbuilders of the nineteenth century. Born in Warren, the son of

George Wesley Bellows's *The Teamster* shows a schooner
in frame on the Camden waterfront in 1916, at the very
end of the era of wooden shipbuilding in Maine.
COLLECTION OF THE FARNSWORTH ART MUSEUM, ROCKLAND
BEQUEST OF MRS. ELIZABETH B. NOYCE, 1997

an Irish immigrant, O'Brien went to sea before apprenticing to
a local shipwright. At his death in 1882, aged eighty-eight,
O'Brien had owned and built ships for six decades in the course
of which he had become the country's fourteenth millionaire.

Square rig had all but vanished from the coasting trades, but
it was still profitable for carrying bulk cargoes on long voyages—
principally grain, which had proved to be of greater long-term
significance to California than gold. Although it took a few years
for Maine shipbuilders to recover from the war, in 1870 they
launched twenty-four ships, barks, or barkentines—more than
half of those built in the whole country—and five years later
fifty-four of the country's seventy-nine square-rigged vessels. If
clippers were built for speed, the Down Easter was built for
capacity. But the spirit of experiment and improvement that

informed the clipper age was not forgotten, and many Down Easters were considered medium clippers and they could hold their own rolling round the Horn to 'Frisco. Down Easters are distinguished from the clippers in another way: their names are more prosaic. While the owner of a sleek new clipper might name it for a Native American chief, opera singer, or weather phenomenon, the Down Easter was more often than not named for a man of business or his relative.

The case of O'Brien's Thomaston fleet is illustrative. All of the fourteen ships fully owned by him between 1858 and 1882 were named for people: two for himself, four for relatives, two for political figures, and five for merchants and shipmasters, including the *Baring Brothers* (2,090 tons, 244 feet) and the *John Bryce* (1,968 tons, 220 feet) named for a principal in the Callao, Peru, firm of Bryce, Grace & Co. Baring Brothers and Company was one of the leading banking houses of the late nineteenth century. They happened to have considerable interests in South America, especially in Peru, which was one of the major sources of guano or bird droppings. A phosphate- and nitrogen-rich fertilizer, guano was one of the major cargoes for square-riggers in the last decades of commercial sail. Freighting bulk cargoes such as guano and grain remained competitive only so long as the ships could be run more economically than steamships on the same routes. In the twilight of the age of wooden ships and iron men, the domineering spirit of "bully captains and bucko mates" drove the Down Easter crews hard, and shipwrights built more efficient ships that could carry ever larger cargoes with ever smaller crews.

If there is a single vessel that marks the transition from the Down Easter to the final era of commercial square rig, it is probably the Kennebunk-built four-masted bark *Ocean King*. Launched in 1874, *Ocean King* was not the first vessel so rigged, but she was the first so rigged in the interest of economy. The largest sailing ship afloat when launched (2,516 tons, 250 feet), she carried square sails on her first three masts, and was fore-and-aft on the fourth mast, called a spanker or jigger. Four- and even five-masted full-rigged ships were technically possible, and a few were built, but though they require significantly larger crews, the increased sail area does not result in a commensurate gain in speed. To remain competitive against the rising tide of steam, ships had to be efficient and fast.

One way to do that was through a disciplined crew, and officers needed to be tough, in part because it was a tough trade to begin with, and also because the forecastles of deepwater ships the world over were inhabited by people of widely different backgrounds and abilities, and all too often "shanghaied." (The term originated on the San Francisco waterfront where prospective crew were sometimes drugged by crimps before being signed on against their will for voyages to China and beyond.) In the late

Builder of the last great fleet of American square-riggers, Arthur Sewall (second from left) is seen here aboard the four-masted *Shenandoah* with the white-shirted Captain James F. Murphy.
COURTESY MAINE MARITIME MUSEUM, BATH

1890s, the National Seamen's Union of the Pacific published a gruesome document entitled simply the *Red Record*, whose litany of criminal behavior testifies to the extreme lengths that some officers were willing to go. In all, the *Red Record* examines sixty-four cases of unnecessary cruelty and murder aboard American ships in the Cape Horn trade between 1888 and 1895. Whatever the reason, shipboard discipline needed an enforcer. As veteran Cape Horner and author Captain Felix Riesenberg described him:

...THE FIGURE of the bucko mate, belaying-pins in his short boots and knuckle dusters on his fists, comes back out of the past, not as an adjunct to morbid romance but as a cruel fact. He broke men and killed them on the cruel blue sea without the aid of fire.

One of the last of her breed, the wooden four-masted bark *Susquehannah*, riding light in the Kennebec after her launching in 1891.
COURTESY MAINE MARITIME MUSEUM, BATH

Some officers with "the advantage of position, a high morale built up through years of command" were more restrained. As his ship lay at anchor in Manila in 1898, Captain F. C. Duncan and his two mates faced a mutiny led by three of the crew, the remainder of whom stood back to see how things would play out. The captain quickly disarmed the ringleader, and the mates rushed their opponents and "obviously disappointed, received immediate surrenders. There was no brutal follow-up of victory." This eyewitness account was written by Fred Duncan, author of a fascinating memoir about his first twelve years of life sailing the world over with his family aboard the *Florence*, a product of the Goss & Sawyer yard in Bath, "The City of Ships."

Located about twelve miles from the mouth of the Kennebec, the city of Bath has long been at the center of Maine's shipbuilding industry. In its heyday, though many shipyards were clustered in the city, the Bath Customs District included shipyards in cities all along the Kennebec, including Phippsburg, Bath, Richmond, Pittston, Gardiner, Hallowell, and Augusta, as well as Brunswick, Topsham, and Bowdoinham. (Kennebec is an Abnaki word meaning "long, quiet river," which describes an unbroken stretch of river below Augusta.) The Bath district, one of thirteen in the state, accounted for 49,399 of the 172,000 tons of shipping built in Maine in 1853; it was followed closely by Waldoboro, with 40,453 tons, and Portland with 17,549 tons. The financial panic of 1857 resulted in the closing of a number of yards, and in some towns the end of shipbuilding was permanent. For those that survived, the risks to deep-sea commerce from Confederate raiders led to severe cutbacks in the number and size of square-riggers launched, and to an increase in the number of schooners built for coastal trade.

In the 1850s Bath yards launched 12 schooners and 199 square-rigged ships. Three decades later, they launched 255 schooners and only 62 square-riggers. This was the boom decade for schooners, and production declined steadily thereafter: 94 in the next decade, 88 in the 1900s, and only 22 in the 1910s.

Despite some heroic efforts at the end by the yard of Arthur Sewall, the age of the square-rigger was over by 1902. The last of Sewall's wooden square-riggers slid down the ways between 1890 and 1892—*Rappahannock* (3,185 tons, 287 feet), *Shenandoah* (3,407 tons, 298 feet), *Susquehannah* (2,745 tons, 283 feet), and *Roanoke* (3,539 tons, 311 feet).

Like any respectable Down Easter, despite her enormous size—only a handful of wooden vessels ever exceeded her in tonnage—*Roanoke* had a reputation for a good turn of speed. She sailed most frequently in the California grain trade, although she also carried case oil to Shanghai, sugar from Honolulu, and canned fish from Seattle.* On September 5, 1900, she completed a passage from Baltimore to San Francisco with coal. By coincidence, this happened to be the very day that Arthur Sewall died in Maine, and it was also the only time that four Sewall ships were in port together, the other vessels being the steel-hulled *Dirigo*, *Edward Sewall,* and *Erskine M. Phelps.* On the following voyage, from Norfolk for San Francisco, *Roanoke*'s cargo of coal began burning, and the ship was only saved by pouring a continuous stream of water on the coal—and pumping out again—while making for Honolulu, which she reached thirteen days later. In 1904 *Roanoke* was laid up for six months of repairs in Rio de Janeiro after colliding with a British steamer. She then made her way to New Caledonia in the South Pacific to load chrome ore. On August 10, 1905, a fire broke out in the hold and despite the best efforts of her crew, assisted by those of her running mate *Susquehanna* and a Norwegian bark, *Roanoke* was a total loss. Some of her crew shipped aboard *Susquehanna* when she sailed on August 23, only to see that vessel founder three days later. *Rappahannock* had burned a year after her launch, and the sole survivor of the foursome, *Shenandoah*, ended her days as a coal barge before being sunk in a collision off Long Island in 1915.

---

* Case oil was kerosene carried in five-gallon containers packed in a two-container wooden "case."

Originally built as a three-masted ship, the five-masted schooner
Snow & Burgess was immortalized in Burgess Cogill's memoir of her
seafaring childhood, *When God Was an Atheist Sailor.*
COURTESY MAINE MARITIME MUSEUM, BATH

Roanoke was the last wooden ship built by Sewall, but the
yard continued in service for another decade, during which it
built seven steel ships, one steel bark, a barge, and last, in 1903,
a schooner. Sewall was the only American builder of steel-hulled
sailing ships, and his was the only nineteenth-century shipyard
to switch from building wooden vessels to building in steel. The
first in his fleet had actually been the Scottish built *Kenilworth*,
which he brought under the American flag in 1889 only after a
special act of Congress enabled him to do so. After a research
visit to Great Britain, Sewall retooled his shipyard and hired an
English shipwright with experience in steel-hull construction to
oversee the building of *Dirigo*, the name for which—"I lead"—
he aptly borrowed from the state motto. *Dirigo* proved a successful vessel, carrying a variety of bulk and general cargoes on
an even greater variety of routes between the East Coast, West
Coast, Hawaii, Asia, and Europe. Among the ship's more distinguished passengers were Jack London and his wife Charmian.

During their 145-day passage from Baltimore to Seattle, the captain was incapacitated by a fatal stomach ulcer and command of the vessel fell to the first mate, upon whom London later based one of the antagonists in his story, "The Mutiny of the *Elsinore*." Two months after the United States declared war on Germany in 1917, *Dirigo* was sunk by gunfire and scuttling charges placed by the crew of a German U-boat just off the coast of England.

The longest-lived of the Sewall sailing ships of steel was the bark *Kaiulani* of 1900 (1,570 tons, 226 feet), named for the last heiress presumptive to the Hawaiian throne, Princess Victoria Kaiulani. In 1941, loaded with 1.6 million board feet of lumber from the Pacific Northwest, she became the last American square-rigger to round Cape Horn. Cut down to a barge in the Philippines during World War II, she was finally taken to the breakers in 1974.

Not all square-riggers ended as such, and with the declining need for ships and barks on deepwater trade routes, owners began to look for ways to give their vessels a new lease on life. A few underwent a metamorphosis similar to that of the Thomaston-built *Snow & Burgess*. Launched as a three-masted ship in 1878, she worked in the ordinary Down Easter trades for twenty-two years. In 1900–01, she was rerigged first as a bark and then as a five-masted schooner. Over the next fifteen years she hauled lumber from Puget Sound to California, and also coal and wheat along the west coast of the Americas and around Cape Horn to South Africa. The switch to the schooner rig had no adverse affect on her performance, and sometime after 1910 she set a record sailing between Port Ludlow, Washington, and San Francisco. Part of her career is described by Burgess Cogill in her book, *When God Was an Atheist Sailor*, a memoir of the eight years she spent aboard her father's schooner, which she joined on September 5, 1902, at latitude 10°N, longitude 117°W—south of San Diego and west of Costa Rica.

The Schooners

A COMPARISON of the construction figures for square-riggers and schooners in late-nineteenth-century Bath hints at a dramatic development in the evolution of sailing rigs in the last years of commercial sail: the coming of schooners with three or more masts. Because of their smaller size and comparative ease of maintenance, a fair number of two-masted schooners built for freight or the fisheries still survive today, most of them converted to commercial passenger service or in museum ownership either as dockside or working exhibits. The Maine Windjammer Association represents thirteen schooners that have been converted to or built for the passenger trades. Although a few of these are of recent construction, the oldest began their careers in the age of working sail and eight have been designated as National Historic Landmarks because they "possess exceptional value or quality in illustrating and interpreting the heritage of the United States."

The two oldest schooners date from 1871. The *Lewis R. French,* launched at Christmas Cove, and the *Stephen Taber,* built on Long Island, New York, originally carried freight along the

East Coast. As the last wind ships gave way to steam in the years before World War II, Captain Frank Swift founded Maine Windjammer Cruises to keep some of the old schooners at work, and among the first schooners converted to the passenger trade were the *Grace Bailey* (1882), built in Patchogue, New York, which carried freight to the West Indies, and *Mercantile* (1916), built on Little Deer Isle, Maine, to carry salt fish, barrel staves, and firewood. The only pilot schooner built for use in Maine waters, *Timberwind* of 1931, served the port of Portland until 1969, when she was converted for the passenger trade.

The largest vessel in the Maine Windjammer Association fleet is the three-masted centerboard schooner *Victory Chimes* (1900). Built in Bethel, Delaware, she was designed to carry lumber in the shallow waters of Delaware Bay, and she is the last three-masted schooner in service on the East Coast. Three other schooners hail outside of Maine, namely *American Eagle* (1930), a veteran of fifty-three years in the Gloucester fishing fleet, the *Isaac H. Evans* (1886), and the *J. & E. Riggin* (1927), built in Mauricetown and Dorchester, New Jersey, respectively, for the Delaware Bay oyster fisheries.

Although the high-canvassed square-rigged ship was the aristocrat of ocean trade, it is fitting that of the two types it is the more workmanlike and versatile schooner that survives in greater numbers. The relative simplicity of line and rig makes such vessels easy to build and sail. Over the past quarter century more than two dozen new schooners of traditional design have been built both for passenger service and as sail-training vessels. In a tribute to the schooner, maritime historian Howard Chapelle wrote:

> IN SPITE OF the fact that ships and square-riggers monopolized certain important trades, such as the [transatlantic] packet and East Indian, and though they handled large and valuable cargoes individually, the total tonnage and value of such cargoes were small compared to that carried by the schooners in the coasting and foreign trades.

The New England schooner began to evolve as a recognizable form in the early 1700s. Although there is pictorial evidence for schooner-like vessels somewhat earlier, the first known use of the word "schooner" is from a Bostonian account of 1716: "Ye Skooner *Mayflower* from North Carolina." The most common vessels in the coastal trade and fisheries had been the shallop and pinnace, whether rigged with square or fore-and-aft sails. Slightly larger, and sailed more in the offshore fisheries, was the ketch, a term that then described a two-masted, square-rigged vessel. The schooner's great advantage was its predominantly fore-and-aft rig. Coastal passages require a fair amount of tacking and sailing against the wind, and schooners can sail closer to the wind and require far less manpower and skill than a square-rigged vessel of comparable size. Many schooners were also rigged to carry square topsails on the foremast, which gave them a considerable advan-

The last four-masted schooner built on the Kennebunk River, *Kennebunk* was launched from the yard of Charles Ward in 1918, and homeported at Calais, Maine. Courtesy Brick Store Museum, Kennebunk

tage on long downwind passages, as when sailing to and from the West Indies.

Maine shipwrights perfected the art of schooner building early on, especially for the coastwise trades to which American commerce was so often restricted by wars and embargoes. Schooners of the time were ordinarily about 75 feet in length. Although they were not unheard of, two-masted schooners longer than 100 feet were considered dangerous and difficult to man because of their oversized sails, booms, gaffs, and other gear. In the late eighteenth century, Chesapeake Bay shipwrights discovered that it was more efficient to increase the sail area on a larger hull by stepping three masts of ordinary size rather than two masts that were too big to handle safely. The idea did not catch on at first, and fewer than twenty three-masted schooners were launched over the next fifty years, including one at Ellsworth in 1831 and another in nearby Blue Hill two years later. Interest in tern schooners (tern meaning a set of three) picked up just before the Civil War, and over the next seventy-five years or so, approximately 2,250 three-masted schooners were built from Nova Scotia to the Gulf of Mexico, a great many of them in Maine.

Just as the two-masted schooner outgrew its rig, so did the three-master, the largest of which was the *Bradford C. French* (968 tons, 184 feet) launched by David Clark at Kennebunk in 1884. In the never-ending quest for competitive advantage against steamers and trains, schooners continued to grow in size, adding about one mast per decade. The first four-master built as such, the *William L. White* (996 tons, 190 feet), was launched by Goss, Sawyer, and Packard of Bath in 1880; the first five-master on the East Coast, the *Gov. Ames* (1,778 tons, 246 feet), at Waldoboro in 1888; and the first six-master, the *George W. Wells* (2,970 tons, 319 feet), at Camden in 1900. (The singleton seven-master, the *Thomas W. Lawson* (5,218 tons, 385 feet), was built of steel in Massachusetts in 1902.)

The impetus for the sudden interest in large schooners in the last quarter of the nineteenth century was the Northeast's new-found appetite for coal. An increased reliance on steam power for industrial use, for railroads and urban trolley systems, and for generating electricity created a demand that could only be satisfied by bulk shipments of coal from the source of supply. Before the turn of the century, this trade was split between barge carriers whose operations were restricted to relatively sheltered waters like Long Island Sound and Chesapeake Bay, and the coasting schooners, which could sail on the high seas. The richest coal seams were found in western Maryland, whose coal was shipped out of the Potomac River port of Alexandria, Virginia, and in West Virginia. In 1883 the Chesapeake and Ohio Railroad completed a rail link from West Virginia to Norfolk and Newport News, Virginia, on Chesapeake Bay. These rapidly became the two most important coal ports on the East Coast. In time, competition from improved barges and "schooner barges" drove the schooners from their regular routes between Norfolk, New York, and New England. (Schooner barges were sometimes old vessels that carried only stump masts, or sometimes no masts. Tugboats with a 400 horsepower engine could tow a string of as many as

The schooner *John Bracewell* discharging coal at Kennebunkport.
COURTESY BRICK STORE MUSEUM, KENNEBUNK

six at a time.) The last six-masted schooner—and probably the largest wood-hulled sailing vessel ever built—Percy & Small's *Wyoming* (3,730 tons, 329 feet) carried as many as 6,004 tons of coal from Newport News, her primary ports of call being Boston and Portland. By the end of World War I, however, she was no longer profitable on those routes and was forced to sail to St. John, New Brunswick. She was lost with all hands in a March blizzard off Nantucket in 1924.

There is no doubt that the large schooners achieved significant economies of scale. Five-masted schooners averaged about 2,250 tons and six-masters about 3,100 tons. On average, there were about two crewmen per mast, including a mate, an engineer or a cook, plus the captain. A larger vessel or one engaged in longer voyages might sign on more hands, while on smaller vessels the ratio of men to masts was even less. This meant that in the largest schooners, the ratio of tonnage to paid hands could be more than 200-to-1. *Wyoming*'s crew of 13 gave her a ratio of 287 tons per man. By comparison, the Down Easter *Henry B. Hyde* (2,580 tons) sailed with a crew of 34, for a ratio of only 75-to-1. Several schooner masters preferred to sail single-handed, an impressive feat even among schoonermen in the days before engines or motorized winches and capstans. Nonetheless, the search for profits soon rendered the schooners obsolete, and many were cut down to barges.

A few vessels managed to escape the coal trades, at least briefly, the best known example being the five-masted *Edna Hoyt* (1,512 tons, 224 feet), the last of the 58 five-masted schooners built on the East Coast (all but three of them from Maine shipyards). After nine years hauling coal, she began trading between the East Coast and the Caribbean. Her cargoes consisted of general cargo southbound and sheep guano fertilizer from Venezuela or timber from Florida. (During the Florida land boom of the mid-1920s, Maine exported wood to Florida for construction; but there was also a northbound wood trade, including pine from Florida for construction, and dyewoods from the Caribbean.) In August 1937 she loaded a million board feet of lumber at Halifax for Ireland. From Belfast she proceeded to Newport, Wales, to load coal for Venezuela. While lying in Newport, her hull strained when she grounded at low tide and her captain took her to the deeper harbor at Cardiff to complete loading. Sailing November 2, she was severely knocked about in a storm in the Bay of Biscay. The hull damage sustained at Newport proving worse than initially realized, she was taken in tow to Lisbon. Condemned and sold, she ended her days in Portugal much as she might have had she never sailed abroad, as a coal hulk.

Coal was only one of several commodities with which Maine schooners were closely identified in the nineteenth century. Wood in virtually all its forms has been one of the state's primary exports since the colonial era. In the nineteenth century, some of the greatest concentrations of schooners were found at the mouths of the major rivers: Calais on the St. Croix, Machias, Ellsworth on the Union, Bath, and Portland. Most important of all was Bangor, head of ocean navigation on the Penobscot. Founded in 1776 as the Kenduskeag Plantation, the river port didn't come into its own until the lumber industry opened up the incomparable hinterlands drained by the Penobscot, and by the 1840s it was the lumber capital of the world. The industry's growth over the next several decades was astonishing, reaching a peak in 1872 when more than 246 million board feet of lumber were cut. According to an estimate prepared in 1850, the four major tributaries of the Penobscot (the East and West Branches, the Mattawamkeag, and the Passadumkeag) produced 62 million feet of lumber, 19 million laths, as well as shingles, pickets, oars (60,000), and barrel staves. Ten years later, a total of 3,376 ships cleared the port of Bangor, and the river was said to be so thick with ships that one could walk across their decks to Brewer without getting one's feet wet.

Although Bangor's population was only 12,000 people when Henry David Thoreau visited in the 1840s, the city straddled the frontier between worldliness and wilderness,

ITALIAN BARK
LOADING FRUIT BOX
SHOOKS AT BANGOR

The caption to this illustration of the *Leone*—"Italian Bark
Loading Fruit Box Shooks at Bangor"—testifies to the
city's worldly outlook and dependence on the sea in
the nineteenth and early twentieth centuries.
COURTESY MAINE HISTORICAL SOCIETY, PORTLAND

...LIKE A STAR on the edge of night, still hewing at the
forests of which it is built, already overflowing with the lux-
uries and refinements of Europe, and sending its vessels to
Spain, to England, and to the West Indies for its groceries,
and yet only a few axe-men have gone "up river," into the
howling wilderness which feeds it....

Those who did go "up river" used the bateau, "a sort of mon-
grel between the canoe and the boat," which French trappers
adapted for river transportation early on. The bateaux of Thoreau's day differed little, if at all, from the craft that carried
Arnold's men up the Kennebec and down the Chaudière during
their march on Quebec:

THEY ARE light and shapely vessels, calculated for rapid
and rocky streams, and to be carried over long portages on
men's shoulders, from twenty to thirty feet long, and only
four or four and a half wide, sharp at both ends like a canoe,
though broadest forward on the bottom and reaching seven
or eight feet over the water, in order that they may slip over
rocks as gently possible.... They told us that one wore out
in two years, or often in a single trip, on the rocks....

As they had been for the Royal Navy's mast cutters, the rivers
were crucial to the lumbermen not only because they provided
easy access to the interior for the canoes and bateaux that carried
work crews and supplies, but also for moving the logs to the
mills. Hauled to streams or lakes in the dead of winter, the logs
would begin the drive downriver with the spring freshets.* At

---

* Freshet: a stream or river flood caused by the spring thaw or heavy rain.

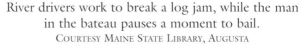

River drivers work to break a log jam, while the man
in the bateau pauses a moment to bail.
COURTESY MAINE STATE LIBRARY, AUGUSTA

Moving a log boom aross a lake by means of a
headworks—tough work.

the end of the drive on the Penobscot, the logs in their thousands would be sorted for milling at the Old Town mills, and then loaded on ships in Bangor. Seventeen miles downriver they entered Penobscot Bay between Bucksport and Fort Knox, the largest fort in Maine and a powerful reminder of the river's importance to the nation.

On the lakes, where there was no current, huge rafts of logs were corralled by booms (logs joined together end-to-end) and moved forward by means of a headworks—a raft-mounted capstan—in a procedure that sailors call kedging. An anchor weighing 200 or 300 pounds was taken in a bateau and dropped some distance from the raft. As the crew of the raft hauled the warp in around the capstan, the raft moved to the position of the anchor, which was taken in so that the procedure could be repeated. In fair weather, a large boom might be moved one or two miles per day via a headworks. A headwind could easily drive a raft backwards or worse break it up entirely. This backbreaking labor was eased somewhat on Moosehead Lake with the arrival of the steamer *Amphitrite* in 1844. Five years later *Moosehead* towed a log raft that reportedly covered twenty-one acres of lake. Forty miles long and eighteen miles across at its widest, Moosehead Lake lies about 1,000 feet above sea level and forms the headwaters of the Kennebec.

Construction was one of the primary uses for lumber, and as the production figures for Bangor attest, Americans were profligate consumers. Although wood was cheap and easy to use, as cities grew denser, municipal authorities worried about the risk of fire. In Maine alone, major fires devastated Portland (1866), Bangor (1911), and Bar Harbor (1947). Thanks in part to new building codes specifying the use of brick and stone, Brewer became a major manufacturer and exporter of bricks, which were renowned for their quality. According to the specifications in some government contracts, buildings had to be "constructed of Brewer brick or equal." Situated across the Penobscot from Bangor, Brewer is built on a land rich in clay. Local makers fired their brick with the scrap wood from the Old Town and Bangor mills, and skippers were happy to carry brick because wood is a relatively light cargo and the denser bricks made good ballast.

The Penobscot region was the source of two other major building products in the 1800s, both concentrated at the lower end of the Bay: lime and granite. Lumbering and fishing, the twin engines of Maine's resource economy today, are still two of the most dangerous occupations in the United States, but they were nothing as compared with Maine's lime industry. A major ingredient of mortar and plaster, lime is a powder made by burning limestone, a calcium-rich sedimentary rock formed of the decomposed remains of plankton and other aquatic organisms. In Maine, limestone is found chiefly in a narrow stretch of land from Thomaston to Camden. (Only a few miles from the current shoreline, this area used to be submerged beneath the Gulf of Maine.) The center of the lime industry—lime burning, shipbuilding, and shipping—was Rockland, which until 1848 was a part of Thomaston called Shore Village. There was also considerable activity in nearby Rockport and Camden. Produced and exported to Boston as early as 1733, lime was exploited on a large scale by General Henry Knox, who settled at Thomaston after the American Revolution. The primary markets for lime were Boston, New York, and, closer by, Bangor and Portland.

Lime is extremely flammable when mixed with water, which also causes it to expand. This makes carrying lime by sea a dicey business under the best of circumstances. Despite the extensive precautions taken to prevent water reaching the casks, either through openings in the deck or from the bilge, the incidence of fire aboard limers was all too high. As lime is also used to make mortar, if a fire did occur and did not immediately threaten the safety of the ship, a cask of lime would be opened and used to caulk any holes that might admit air into the hold. Burning or smoldering limers were not allowed in port, and they could not anchor near other vessels in case the fire spread. Often if a fire could not be smothered and it was close enough to shore, the crew would run the schooner into shallow water and open the hull below the waterline at low tide. When the tide returned, the water would extinguish the fire, but it would also cause the lime to expand and the casks and hull would burst from the pressure.

Because of the dangers inherent in freighting lime, insurance was hard to come by, and lime schooners tended to be "old tubs...which are always getting afire and making trouble." Some schooners were built as such, with a false bottom above the bilge so that the bottom tier of casks would have less chance of being infiltrated by water. In 1900 the newly formed Rockland-Rockport Lime Company introduced iron barges capable of carrying 16,000 barrels each. The lime captains denounced the purchase as a "most cold-blooded, shameless barefaced attempt to depreciate or destroy the value of the property of their neighbors." It didn't matter. The Rockland lime industry was in steep decline, and within a decade or two, wallboard, concrete, and plywood had rendered the lime industry an unprofitable business.

Lime burning required tens of thousands of cords of wood

per year, and as the woodlots around Thomaston and Rockland were soon exhausted, there grew up an amorphous mass of ships known as the kilnwood fleet, worn-out vessels whose crews scavenged the coast in search of wood to fuel the lime kilns. As suitable wood became scarce along the lower end and islands of Penobscot Bay in the 1870s, the kilnwooders began to go farther afield, to the Penobscot River where they combed for scoots, or refuse wood, to Machias, and ultimately New Brunswick. The last was famous for its "Johnny woodboats," slab-sided schooners sporting a cat schooner rig (two gaff-rigged masts, the foremast set well forward, and no headsails), and with a "barn door" rudder, so called for the way it looked mounted to the flat transom. Hastily built, often by farmers working in the off-season,

Scouring the coast for fuel as far as New Brunswick, lumber schooners delivered thousands of tons of cordwood to feed the Rockland lime kilns. COURTESY MAINE MARITIME MUSEUM, BATH

these vessels routinely sailed with their gunwales awash on the assumption that wood would float whether it was an integral part of the hull itself or simply a well-attached cargo.

Another nineteenth-century industry centered on Penobscot Bay was granite quarrying, which had a great impact especially on the islands. Granite is also found farther up the coast in Hancock County, around Deer Isle and Blue Hill, and inland on the Kennebec around Hallowell. Although it is now almost uninhabited, in its heyday, Dix Island, off Rockland, had a population of more than 2,000 people. One of the most significant quarry operations was located on Vinalhaven, Maine's largest offshore island. For more than a century—the 1820s to the 1930s—granite was one of the island's primary industries, and the year-round population reached more than 2,800 people, twice what it is today. Cutters, polishers, and shapers immigrated from around the United States, the British Isles, Italy, and Scandinavia, to shape stone for construction projects around the country, in cities as far apart as Pensacola, St. Louis, Omaha, Buffalo, and even San Francisco. The roster of projects for which Maine granite was used is impressive, and includes coastal fortifications, museums, customs houses and post offices, the base of the Brooklyn Bridge, Chicago's Union Station and Board of Trade, monuments, and a variety of federal office buildings in the nation's capital.

One of the islanders' more impressive feats was the cutting and shaping of the eight pillars that form the choir of the Cathedral of St. John the Divine in New York City, by some measures the largest Gothic cathedral in the world. Each pillar measures 54.6 feet high and 8 feet in diameter at the base, weighs 120 tons, and is formed of only two pieces, the taller one being about 36 feet high. With the rise of structural steel and concrete as building materials after the turn of the century, the granite industry declined quickly, although quarries for paving granite—which can be found under foot in cities from Portland to Philadelphia—remained active into the 1930s.

Although special barges were employed to carry the "eight columns of worship" from Vinalhaven to New York, the primary vehicles for shipping granite long distances were schooners. For short-haul freighting, stone sloops were employed, gaff-rigged vessels with a single mast to which was attached a boom derrick for lifting the stone. A great many of these were owned on Chebeague Island, the largest island in Casco Bay. The stone sloops of Chebeague averaged about 60 feet in length with a length-to-beam ratio of about 3-to-1, and a draft of only 5 feet, a shape that provided a stable platform for loading and carrying the granite and that enabled them to work close inshore. Although there were some schooners involved in the granite trade, the advantage of the sloop rig was that it kept the decks clear, which made handling the stone easier and safer. Because there was only one mast, the stone sloops set gargantuan mainsails: that on the *M. M. Hamilton* (111 tons, 90 feet), the largest of the stone sloops, was 1,003 square yards—almost a quarter of an acre.

In the late 1700s stone sloops were used primarily to carry ballast for ships being built around Casco Bay. As the granite industry developed after the War of 1812, the sloops grew in size. While some sloops are remembered for their work on some of the more historic projects of the day—the *M. M. Hamilton* carried stone for the Washington Monument—in general they found employment in more prosaic tasks such as freighting paving blocks and cellar stone, and carrying grout, or filler stone, for lighthouses and harbor improvements. The Rockland breakwater was a typical project, although somewhat larger than most as the breakwater extends about three-quarters of a mile out from shore. The work is described in *The Stone Sloops of Chebeague*:

> ...GRANITE WAS being taken from Fox Island, Vinal Haven, Spruce Head, etc. and ferried to the site of the Breakwater where it was dropped into the sea—the depth at low tide was often over 40 feet. Several Chebeague stone sloops were doing the work, and it was not unusual to have six or

eight sloops strung along either side of where the breakwater was being built, letting go their stone.

The huge blocks of granite, often weighing six to ten
tons, would be swung overside by the boom derrick and
then dropped.... Naturally when such a weight was sud-
denly gone, the sloop lurched, and rocked violently—the
dogs, boom derrick, the sail boom and gaff, lines, blocks—
everything swung in every direction—"you ran for your
life, they could cut you in two."

Although it occupied only a small portion of the carrying
trade for Maine schooners, one of the more interesting cargoes
exported from the state was ice. In the days before electrical re-
frigeration, ice was a precious commodity that found ready markets throughout the United States, especially in the south, as
well as in the West Indies and farther abroad. Ice could be harvested on any body of frozen fresh water, but in the late 1800s

Loading ice at the Maine Ice Company plant in West Boothbay,
Maine, February 22, 1907. The photograph was taken aboard the
General E. S. Greeley; the five-masted schooner *Magnus Manson*
is seen at right. Courtesy Maine Maritime Museum, Bath

the center of the ice trade was on the Kennebec River between the top of Merrymeeting Bay and Augusta. (The Kennebec is tidal all the way to Augusta, but the limit of saltwater ends just above Bath.) When the ice was at least one foot thick, operations would begin to cut it into blocks 12 by 22 inches square.* These were stored in icehouses that lined the river until the spring melt. Ice was carefully loaded into the ships and packed around with a dunnage of ice chips and hay, coarse sawdust, or wood shavings. Despite the fact that ice carriers often sailed into very warm climates, the rate of loss from melting or evaporation was usually no more than 30 percent. (In 1833 a Boston ship loaded 180 tons of ice for India. When it arrived, after twice crossing the equator, 100 tons of ice remained.) The Thomaston-built four-masted schooner *Mabel Jordan* (994 tons, 181 feet) made annual voyages with ice to Rio de Janeiro. Although there were profits to be made, some ship owners refused to carry ice because the freshwater melt could rot the hull.

The age of sail left an apparently indelible mark on the coast of Maine, and schooners especially held out longer than they did in other parts of the country. A variety of conditions enabled them to find profitable opportunities even as steam engines in both ships and trains captured the majority of the carrying trades in the last quarter of the 1800s. Although schooners and square-riggers gave steam power a run for its money, both sail and steam would ultimately lose out to the internal combustion engine in the age of the car and the truck.

---

* An acre of ice 12 inches thick netted about 1,000 tons of marketable ice before shipping.

A Century of Progress

HOWEVER dangerous the work performed by stone sloops and other craft in creating the infrastructure necessary for safe navigation, such improvements as breakwaters, wharves, and lighthouses were absolutely essential to Maine's progress as a maritime state in the 1800s. It was in that century that the bulk of this work was done, and when the returns appeared the greatest because more people were dependent on maritime industries. If the building of Portland Head Light in 1790 reflected the government's faith in the commercial potential of the port, the lighthouse building program in the two decades following statehood in 1820 was a clear indication of Maine's importance as a center of merchant shipping and shipbuilding.

Of the sixty-three lighthouses still standing in 2000, eight were in commission by 1817, thirty-seven were built between 1820 and 1859, and the others were lit between 1870 and 1909. Maine's second lighthouse was built in 1797 on Seguin Island. Located just off the mouth of the Kennebec River, it can be a challenging island to circumnavigate because of the difficult conditions that prevail on the north side of the island when the wind blows counter to the ebbing tide. Recognizing the importance of the light not just to guide mariners through the approaches to the Kennebec and Sheepscot Rivers, but also to help them along the coast, in the 1850s the light was fitted with a first-order Fresnel lens, the most powerful made, measuring six feet in diameter. Similar offshore beacons are strung across the mouths of Muscongus and Penobscot Bays to Mount Desert Island—on Monhegan Island (1824), Matinicus (1827), and Mount Desert Rock (1830). A shard of dirtless granite fifteen miles offshore, the latter is considered the most exposed lighthouse in the United States.

Almost as remote is Matinicus Rock, located six miles south of Matinicus Island. This lighthouse achieved a degree of fame thanks to the redoubtable Abbie Burgess, the daughter of the

Andrew Winter's *Seguin Island Light* (1940).
COLLECTION OF THE FARNSWORTH ART MUSEUM, ROCKLAND
GIFT OF MR. AND MRS. LEO MEISSNER

lighthouse keeper there in the mid-1800s. When she was seventeen, her father went ashore for supplies but was kept from returning by a storm that raged a full month. During that time, Burgess looked after her younger sisters and her frail mother, and maintained the light every night even as the house in which they lived was flooded by waves that crashed over the island and "the only endurable places were the light towers." Recalling the events of that winter, she wrote to a friend: "You have often expressed a desire to view the sea out upon the ocean when it was angry. Had you been here on the 19 January, I surmise you would have been satisfied." Burgess later married Isaac H. Grant and two years after he was assigned to Whitehead Light in Tenants Harbor, the Bureau of Lighthouses formally recognized, and compensated, Abbie Burgess for her services as assistant light keeper, a post she held until her retirement in 1890.

While the federal government ensured the safety of saltwater navigation, private enterprise and the state did all they could to stimulate Maine's economy from within. The difficulty of land transportation, the importance of seaports, and the abundance of natural waterways made canals an obvious means to facilitate the movement of goods and people around the state. The logging industry was the first to "improve" rivers by building catch basins to create waterpower for mills, and building dams to raise the water level on small streams so that logs could be floated into larger rivers. From such experience came one of the more sophisticated and long-lasting canals built in the state, the Telos Cut, which lasted from 1838 to 1921. Although the cut between Telos and Webster Lakes northwest of Baxter State Park can be measured in the hundreds of yards, its utility was guaranteed only by the construction of dams on Churchill, Chamberlain, and Eagle Lakes. By damming the headwaters of the Allagash River at Chamberlain Lake and raising the water level so that it overflowed into the East Branch of the Penobscot River, Bangor lumbermen could drive their logs to the Old Town mills rather than to St. John, New Brunswick, via the Allagash and St. John Rivers.

Of greater significance to the more inhabited parts of the state were the attempts to build canals on the New Meadows, Mousam, Georges, Saco, and Androscoggin Rivers. Built in 1791 and operational for only two years, the New Meadows Canal led from the headwaters of the New Meadows River to the Kennebec.[*] Engineering difficulties and lack of adequate capital prevented the builders from fully realizing their vision, which was to bring lumber from the Kennebec watershed to the sawmills of eastern Casco Bay near Brunswick and Freeport. The most successful of the Maine canals, the Cumberland and Oxford (C & O) Canal (1830–70), formed a continuous waterway from Harrison at the top of Long Lake, through the town of Naples, through a lock on the Songo River (still in service) to Sebago Lake, from there to the Presumpscot River and down to Portland via locks and short lengths of man-made cuts. As originally proposed, the canal was to have extended from Harrison to Waterford in Oxford County (hence its name), and there were various proposals to extend the C & O as far as Bethel, with a connection to the Androscoggin River, but the canal fell short of its promoters' expectations and such expansion was out of the question. Although farmers came from as far away as New Hampshire to sell goods into the Portland market, ice closed the canal up to four months each year (one store's records show monthly orders for one barrel of rum, except for November when five were needed), passenger traffic was virtually nonexistent, and what markets it did serve were increasingly diverted to the railroads starting in the 1850s.

Cargo vessels designed for work on the rivers and canals were distinct from the nimble rapids-friendly craft of the lumbermen. On the C & O Canal, the Kennebec River, and especially the Pis-

[*] "The New Meadows River is the only river draining into eastern Casco Bay. It is relatively short, but of all the Casco Bay rivers it is the widest, deepest, and most navigable. In fact, the term river is almost a misnomer. It drains only a small area, saltwater reaches almost to the river's headwaters, and practically all of the water passing in and out of the river is tidal." Rindlaub, *Maine Coast Guide*, p. 205.

cataqua River, barge-like craft called "gundalows" were the most common carriers from the colonial period until the early 1900s. Novelist Sarah Orne Jewett, who lived on the Piscataqua at South Berwick wrote:

> WHEN YOU catch sight of a tall lateen sail, and a strange clumsy craft that looks heavy and low in the water, you will like to know that its ancestor was copied from a Nile boat, from which a sensible old sea captain took a lesson in shipbuilding many years ago.

Jewett's cosmopolitan musings notwithstanding, the gundalow's origins are obscure. The word itself is a corruption of the Italian "gondola," although the only shared characteristic is that both vessels can be poled. The exact rig and form of the gundalow varied considerably, but one feature they had in common was that the mast or boom (in the case of the lateen rig which Jewett describes) could be "jackknifed" easily when passing under

The lake steamer *Goodridge* (1913–32) entering the lock on the Songo River between Sebago Lake and Long Lake.
COURTESY MAINE HISTORICAL SOCIETY, PORTLAND

A two-masted gaff-rigged canal boat on Sebago Lake. The masts were mounted on deck in tabernacles, enabling the crew to lower the masts quickly when passing under bridges.
COURTESY MAINE HISTORICAL SOCIETY, PORTLAND

bridges. Kennebec gundalows set square sails—sometimes on two masts—which could, with a fair wind, carry them upriver against the current above Augusta. Like the Venetian gondola, however, the shallow-draft gundalow was designed to be poled and it often was, when the wind was insufficient or when traversing narrow canals.

The Kennebec gundalows were often referred to simply as longboats. Measuring 60 to 90 feet long, 15 to 20 feet broad, the largest could carry as much as 100 tons of cargo. Some were fitted with "a booth at one end very convenient for the transportation of families as well as goods." Mrs. Jeremiah Chaplin was describing her 1818 journey with her husband, children, and seven theological students to Waterville, where they established what became Colby College. Longboats remained in business on the middle Kennebec, between Augusta and Waterville, until the introduction of steam navigation in the 1830s. But as early as 1822, separate steamboat service was envisioned using modified gundalows between Hallowell and Waterville, and Bath and Augusta. Two gundalows were built, or retrofitted, with steam–driven paddle wheels. Neither achieved their potential, and the middle Kennebec wouldn't open to steam navigation until the 1840s. One of the early steamers, the underpowered *Kennebec*, was sold to Portland interests. A second *Kennebec* (87 tons, 81 feet) was built at Bath in 1823 and offered service between Portland and Bath for nearly a decade. Like riverboats everywhere, these boats drew very little water. Designed to ride over the shallows and falls the length of the river, they were said to "float in a thick fog" and to travel "cross country in a heavy autumn dew."

At the same time that coastwise trade was increasing in the 1820s and 1830s, steam vessels were carving out an ever greater share of the trade traditionally reserved for schooners, especially scheduled passenger and packet service. Far from recoiling at the prospect of steam navigation, many in Maine embraced it. The world's first commercially successful steamboat, Robert Fulton's *North River Steamboat,* entered service at New York in 1807. Seven years later, Jonathan Morgan, "a well-known and eccentric citizen of Portland, Maine," built a steamboat on the Sheepscot at Alna, "having never seen any steam machinery, nor drawing, nor description." Although a second engine moved the un-named craft at four knots, neither this nor a new vessel built at Brunswick can be viewed as anything more than a demonstration of steam power.

The first successful steamer on the Kennebec was the Bath-built *Waterville* (87 tons, 82 feet) launched from King's yard in 1823. As the name suggests, this was intended to be part of a steamer service that would connect her namesake to the lower Kennebec below the falls at Augusta. In fact it would be nine years before *Ticonic* entered service between Waterville, Augusta, and, when the water was high enough, Gardiner. When a lock and dam opened at Augusta in 1836, it was too small for *Ticonic*, although a steamer called *Tom Thumb* and other smaller vessels maintained service to Waterville. There are doubts as to when the *Tom Thumb* arrived on the Kennebec, and it may be that contemporary records refer to two different vessels of the same name. There certainly was a 30-ton paddle steamer built in New York in 1824 that sailed between Eastport and Calais or St. John, New Brunswick. This *Tom Thumb* also served on different routes before stranding on Boon Island, off York in southern Maine, on October 29, 1836, without loss of life. (Not all shipwrecks on Boon Island have ended so well. In December 1710 the merchant ship *Nottingham Galley* sank off barren Boon Island. The fourteen survivors lived on uncooked shellfish and seabirds, and the body of "the old carpenter," before they were rescued after twenty-four days. The ship's captain and first mate wrote differing accounts of the experience, which only ten men survived, upon which the novelist Kenneth Roberts based his account of the tragedy, *Boon Island*. The wreck site was excavated in 1995 and the artifacts recovered included nine of the ship's iron guns.)

Early steamboats were plagued by explosions and fires, a fact that enabled Maine interests to start service to the Penobscot at a relatively low cost. During the summer of 1823, five men were killed when an engine on the new steamer *Patent* exploded during the builder's trials on the Hudson River. The bad publicity forced her owners to sell her out of the New York market, and the Kennebec Steam Navigation Company bought *Patent* at a discount. In August 1823 she inaugurated service between Boston, Portland, and Bath, connecting at the last port with *Waterville*. The next year, the catamaran steamer *Maine* brought weekly service to Bangor via Boothbay, Waldoboro, Owl's Head, Camden, Belfast, Castine, and Bucksport.

Mechanical failure was a cause of many steamer accidents, but human error played a role in many otherwise avoidable accidents. One of the more horrifying disasters in Maine waters involved the New Brunswick-built *Royal Tar*. In September 1836 the "fine substantial-built boat" was en route from St. John to Portland with a cargo that included a traveling zoo. According to a report filed by John Anderson, Collector of Customs in Portland, while the ship was crossing Penobscot Bay, "the keepers of the animals began to feed them, which novelty, it is supposed, drew the attention of the engineer and firemen in charge from their duty." In the hands of an inexperienced junior fireman, the untended boilers overheated and the deck caught fire. The captain anchored *Royal Tar* in an effort to bring the situation under control but the firefighting pumps were in the wrong location and there was a gale blowing, which made the fire burn harder. Most of the crew and passengers were rescued thanks to the help of the USRC *Veto*, but all the animals were lost.

Such tragedies were the exception rather than the rule, and the passenger steamer *Bangor* established a name for herself as the first American steamer to cross the Atlantic under steam power alone, and the first to operate on three continents. The first steamship to cross the Atlantic was the bark-rigged paddle steamer *Savannah* in 1819. The validity of this claim has been challenged on the grounds that she proceeded chiefly under sail and only fired her engines a few times. The earliest steamships were not designed to sail transatlantic, principally because they couldn't carry enough fuel for the inefficient engines then in use. Several European vessels made the westward passage (and some round-trip voyages) after 1819, but the first U.S.-built vessel to cross the Atlantic under steam alone was the New York-built *Bangor* (385 tons, 156 feet). Ordered for the Boston and Bangor Steamship Company in 1834, she served on that route with stops at Portland and other intermediate ports for eight years. Outmoded and facing competition from both railroads and other steamboats, she was transferred to the Portland-Calais run before being sold to the Turkish government. In August 1842 she steamed for Halifax at the start of a two-month voyage that ended in Istanbul. Renamed *Sudaver*, she sailed as a passenger ferry crossing the Sea of Marmora between Asia and Europe—the first American steamer to operate on three continents. She reportedly stayed in service until the 1880s.

It is interesting to note that the initiative for Maine's extensive steamship operations came from Maine and that "Boston had no steamboat facilities until 1824, when a Maine corporation established a line from Boston 'down East.'" Between 1836 and 1860 Maine shipyards built 57 steamers, three more than in Massachusetts, and in the latter year the number of people in Maine claiming "steamboatman" as an occupation was 33, compared with only 11 in Massachusetts. New York boasted 295 working a total of 205,000 tons of steamers registered in the state, which included extensive steamboat operations on the Hudson River and the Great Lakes.

The availability of such expertise helped establish Portland in the competitive steamship trade. One of the more important developments for Maine commerce was the development of Portland as a port of call for transatlantic steamers on fixed schedules. In this the city benefited from the fact that it is closer to Europe than Boston and New York, and from Canada's need for an ice-free port accessible to Quebec. In the mid-1840s Bangor lawyer John A. Poor determined to connect Maine to the network of railroads springing up around the country. In particular, he thought that Portland could become the winter port for Quebec. He also envisioned an integrated freight system that would connect Europe and America via train and ship, a concept first articulated by British engineer and designer Isambard Kingdom Brunel, who in 1837 built the steamship *Great Western* for just such a service. To that end Poor formed the Atlantic and St. Lawrence Railway, and Canadian interests formed the St. Lawrence and Atlantic Railway, to build a railroad between Portland and Montreal. The two companies folded shortly before the international railroad line opened in 1856. The line was taken over by Canada's Grand Trunk Railroad, later the Canadian National Railroad, almost immediately. At the same time, the short-lived Canadian Steam Navigation Company started wintertime service to Portland in 1853. Within a few years this had been absorbed by the Allen Line, which maintained service to

Portland for decades, one of the more common routes being from Liverpool via Queenstown (Cork) where the ships embarked thousands of Irish emigrants. The great advantage to Canada was the ability to export grain, and Grand Trunk grain elevators towered over the Portland waterfront at the foot of Munjoy Hill.

In 1846 Poor had founded the Portland Company on the Fore River, only a few blocks from what would become the Grand Trunk terminal, to build steam engines for the trains on his Atlantic and St. Lawrence Railway. Over the years the company branched out considerably, building marine engines, 160 ships, and even automobiles in the early twentieth century. Unfortunately the ship with which it is most often associated is the side-wheel passenger steamer *Portland*. As is usual in building powered vessels, the hull and engine plant were built by different contractors. The New England Shipbuilding Corporation in

Fr. Goth's *The Arrival of the Steamship* Oregon *at Portland, Maine, on January 21, 1884* shows passengers disembarking at the Grand Trunk Wharves near the foot of Hancock Street.
COURTESY PEABODY ESSEX MUSEUM, SALEM, MASSACHUSETTS

Bath built the hull, Bath Iron Works the boilers, and the Portland Company the engines. Commissioned by the Portland Steam Packet Company for its overnight service to Boston, the handsome, well-found steamer worked on that run without incident for eight years.

On the evening of November 26, 1898, the Saturday after Thanksgiving, *Portland* sailed from Boston with about 192 passengers and crew aboard. Although the Portland Steam Packet Company later claimed to have wired Captain Hollis H. Blanchard to postpone her departure, in view of the weather prudence should have dictated a delay. Many other ships scheduled to depart New England ports that night postponed their departures. Several vessels and light keepers later reported seeing *Portland* in Massachusetts Bay, but the following night, remains of the ship and her passengers began washing ashore along the eastern shore of Cape Cod. It is believed that the ship made it as

The passenger steamer *City of Rockland* leaving the Eastern Steamship Dock at Belfast, Maine, in 1908.
COURTESY MAINE MARITIME MUSEUM, BATH

far north as Cape Ann when her engines were partially disabled. Blown eastward across Massachusetts Bay, *Portland* foundered five to twenty miles north of Provincetown. The exact number of dead—including a disproportionate number of people from Portland's African-American community—was never determined because the only passenger manifest went down with the ship. (As a result of this tragedy, ships were subsequently required to leave a copy of the passenger manifest ashore before sailing.) Although some 400 boats and ships of various descriptions were lost along the coast that night—the majority of them in port— the storm has always been referred to as the *Portland* Gale.

Ironically, for all Maine's efforts to capitalize on the development of the railroads, it was the railroads that proved Maine's undoing as they reoriented the traditional flow of people and freight from a north-south coastal axis to an east-west transcontinental one. Canadian interest even prevailed over Maine's dominant railway system when they opened direct rail links between Montreal, Quebec, and the ice-free ports of St. John in 1871 and Halifax in 1876. The feeder line for both of these ran through Bangor. Apart from the lines built to serve Canadian interests, most of the railroads that reached Maine ran up from the south.

That Mainers continued to build and sail schooners and other sailing vessels in Maine well into the twentieth century suggests to many a conservative nostalgia for tradition in the face of inexorable progress. In fact the United States as a whole came late to iron and steel shipbuilding—about a quarter century after the British in iron hulls, somewhat less in steel—and iron shipbuilding was clustered along the Delaware River in Pennsylvania and Delaware, close to the sources of supply of the needed metals. Shipbuilders and merchants of Maine have long paid scrupulous attention to the bottom line. Shipyards continued to build in wood after it was profitable to do so elsewhere because it made sound business sense. There was an abundance of skilled labor, and wood was relatively plentiful, although a good deal of shipbuilding timber had to be imported from southern states. And

Built at Bath Iron Works, the gunboat *Machias* is seen here in dry-
dock at the Charlestown Navy Yard, Boston, in October 1899.

in building their great five- and six-masted schooners, the Bath
firm of Percy & Small imported Douglas-fir masts from Oregon,
a dramatic indication of how thorough lumber interests had
been in clearing the Maine woods over the course of two centuries. The last burst of schooner building came during World
War I, and between 1916 and 1918 the firm of Crowell & Thur-
low, managing owners of Thomaston's Atlantic Coast Company
shipyard, among others, paid its shareholders dividends of 147
percent. In World War II, twenty-five years later, twenty different boat- and shipyards around the state turned out more than
900 wooden craft of all kinds—from barges, tugs, and work-
boats to coastal minesweepers and sub-chasers—for the Navy,
Army, and U.S. Maritime Commission.

Another factor that contributed to the longevity of wooden shipbuilding in Maine was that it did not require an exorbitant outlay of capital. The costs associated with starting a steel or iron shipyard in 1880 were put at between $200,000 and $1 million—that is ten to fifty times the cost of establishing a wooden shipyard. Despite the daunting financial and logistical obstacles, the Goss Marine Iron Works was founded in 1882 to build marine engines and establish the basis and expertise for an iron shipyard. The company failed, but not before building the first triple-expansion steam engine in the United States. The partners of Goss Marine Iron Works included the shipbuilder Arthur Sewall and Thomas W. Hyde, head of the Bath Iron Works, originally a foundry specializing in marine equipment like bilge pumps and capstans. Hyde purchased the defunct Goss Marine and in 1893 the expanded BIW delivered the steel gunboats *Machias* and *Castine* for the U.S. Navy, followed three years later by the 251-foot-long harbor-defense ram *Katahdin* in 1896.

Named for the highest mountain in Maine, the latter was something of a technological throwback during an era of dramatic change in naval shipbuilding. Rams fitted to the bow of a ship had been one of the principal weapons of galley warfare in antiquity, but in the age of sail ramming had been rendered obsolete in part because of the reliance on wind rather than mechanical propulsion. Steam propulsion seemed to make rams technically feasible again, and in 1882 a rear admiral proposed one for coastal defense against European ironclads. The Navy was not easily convinced, and it took more than a decade to have funds appropriated for a single experimental vessel. *Katahdin*'s primary armament was the wrought-steel ram itself, although she also mounted four 6-pounder guns. Her double bottom could be flooded to lower the ship about six inches to reduce her already slight profile. This low freeboard made her, in the words of Rear Admiral David Potter, "the most uncomfortable warship ever to fly the American flag." This was due chiefly to the fact that while under way her hatches had to be closed against in-

The ram USS *Katahdin* was ungainly and impractical, but visually distinctive. Courtesy Maine Maritime Museum, Bath

coming seas, a practice that resulted in temperatures that "attained tropical fervour"—110 degrees in the officers' mess and 125 degrees in the galley, while "the unfortunates who shovelled coal into the fireboxes beneath the boilers smouldered at a height of Fahrenheit I do not venture to name." Decommissioned on October 8, 1898, she ended her days as Ballistic Experimental Target A and was sunk in gunnery trials in Virginia.

The lumber industry introduced steam power to the lakes in the 1840s, and as of 2000, the oldest Bath Iron Works vessel still in commission is the steamer *Katahdin*, homeported in Greenville at the southern tip of Moosehead Lake. Ordered from Bath Iron Works by the Coburn Steamboat Company in 1914, *Katahdin* was prefabricated in sections, disassembled, and taken by rail to Greenville, where it was reassembled and put in service. Since the emergence of Maine's appeal to tourists and "summer people" in the mid-1800s, Moosehead has also been a popular destination for recreational fishermen, and although much of the land is owned by pulp and paper companies, the shoreline is dotted with summer camps great and small. In the late 1800s, more than fifty steamers plied the lake, catering to loggers, summer visitors, and the few farming communities that ringed the lake. *Katahdin*'s dual use was reflected in her construction, with a finely finished upper deck designed for the elegant summer residents, and a more utilitarian lower deck for hauling vehicles, horses, and supplies for the lumber camps. Refitted with diesel engines in the 1920s, she remained in service until 1972 when she was laid up the victim of changes in the logging industry and the preference for cars over boats for transportation. Eventually she was acquired by a non-profit entity which preserved her in working condition, and today she operates as an excursion vessel out of Greenville.

Bath had long been the "City of Ships," but in the later nineteenth and early twentieth centuries its ways of doing business had altered fundamentally. Concentrated capital enabled her shipyards to build ships employing the latest technologies. But she supplied fewer people to crew the ships, and fewer cargoes. Once her ships sailed down the Kennebec, they seldom returned. The transition from dockside town to shipbuilding center was profound and had parallels in other maritime industries, especially the fisheries.

T E N

The Fisheries

*F*OUR HUNDRED years after
Europeans came to the Gulf of Maine in pursuit of cod, fishing
is the state's most conspicuous maritime industry. Although
knowledge of the biology of individual species is increasing, marine ecosystems are so complex that it will be years before scien-
tists and fishermen have a more than superficial understanding
of how individual fisheries work and how they relate to one another. As important as the scientific issues are, technologies,
tastes, politics, and pollution all play significant roles in the Maine
fisheries. There was no commercial lobster industry before the
1840s; today, salt cod is a curiosity. A more dramatic and con-
densed phenomenon was the rise and fall of the sea urchin fishery—the *uni* of Japan's sushi restaurants—which between 1989
and 1994 rose from nothing to a $40 million catch and then col-
lapsed. The decline in catch was matched by a decline in prices
tied to the Japanese economic crisis, a dramatic illustration of
the extent to which Maine fishermen depend on world markets.

The Maine fisheries changed little until about the 1840s. As
they had in the colonial period, two distinct fisheries existed side-

by-side. One was inshore, involving day trips from home or temporary camps as far out as thirty miles, with a return home in the evening. The offshore fisheries required larger boats for extended trips to fishing grounds off Labrador or Newfoundland, with occasional stays on remote shores to dry the catch. In terms of employment, the inshore fisheries were most important because they engaged the efforts of every seacoast village and hamlet on the Maine coast. In the first half of the nineteenth century, the ratio of inshore to offshore fishing vessels was three-, four-, or even five-to-one, depending on the community. The inshore fisheries generally employed smaller boats with smaller crews.[*]

Both the fisheries and fishing methods changed little before the mid-1800s. Fishing for ground fish like cod and haddock was done with a hook and line, a technique called handlining. A fisherman—there were usually four to a boat in the colonial period—lowered a baited hook over the side, and when a fish struck, he hauled it in. The fish were split, gutted, salted, and stowed in the hold. About 1850 there was a switch to dory fishing. Dories are similar to the lumberman's bateau, with which they apparently share a common ancestor. By enabling more fishermen to fish, they made the schooner itself more productive (and its owner or owners richer). But dories made life more difficult and dangerous for the fishermen. Simply launching and retrieving the dories was a chore, and dories were equipped with an oil bag to smooth the waters in the lee of the schooner. The dories themselves were a less stable platform from which to land a 40- to 60-pound cod, much less a halibut weighing several hundred pounds. (Originally regarded as a trash fish, halibut became a commercial species in the 1840s. Today a good-sized halibut runs about 40 pounds.) Dories also had to be rowed to and from the schooner,

---

[*] Maine never developed a whaling industry to speak of. John Smith found the shore "Whalefishing a costly conclusion" and in the nineteenth century only four vessels were fitted out for deepwater whaling: *Science* of Portland, and *Wiscasset* of Wiscasset (1834–41), *Massasoit* of Bath (1841–43), and *Warwick* of Bucksport (1841–42). Some 200 Maine ships were either built for or converted to whaling. See Martin, *Whalemen and Whaleships of Maine.*

and many were lost in sudden gales or fog, or were run down by transatlantic steamers crossing the Banks:

> ...NOTWITHSTANDING the efforts made on board, by the firing of guns, blowing of horns, ringing of bells, and the continued cruising about in search of the missing men, the fact of not being enabled to find them, and being obliged to give up the search and return home is too often the case.

Dory handlining soon gave way to dory trawling, or longlining. A trawl is a long line to which hundreds of shorter hooked lines are attached; colored target buoys marked either end of the long line. After setting the line, the fishermen would row or

Walter Lofthouse Dean's *On the Deep Sea* (1901) shows a two-man dory on the Grand Banks. As one man hauls the halibut aboard, the other keeps his hand on the trawl line. COLLECTION OF THE FARNSWORTH ART MUSEUM, ROCKLAND. GIFT OF MR. AND MRS. JOHN HILL, 1971

sometimes sail the dory back to the end that went into the water first and haul it in, sometimes by means of a roller mounted on the gunwale. As each fish came up the fisherman unhooked the catch, baited the hook, and lowered it over the side. When he had worked his way to the end of the line, he would repeat the process. When the dory was full he returned to the schooner to discharge his catch. Dories and longlines were expensive investments that also required larger, more expensive schooners. An even greater outlay was required for the adoption of the otter trawl, a British invention of the 1890s that revolutionized the way in which ground fish like cod and haddock were caught. An otter trawl is a huge net bag dragged behind a trawler. The mouth of the net is kept open by a complex system of floats at the top, a weighted chain at the bottom, and flat otter boards (also called trawl doors) attached to towing cables that lead to the trawler. As the net is dragged forward, the resistance of the water on the boards forces them to pull in opposite directions, thus keeping the mouth of the net open. Originally designed for bottom dragging, the otter trawl was later adapted for trawling for pelagic species, that is fish that live in the middle of the water column between the surface and the bottom.

In itself, the shift to a capital-intensive fishery represented a dramatic change in the nature of the livelihood, but the economics of the fishing industry changed even more when the codfish bounty was repealed just after the Civil War. When Congress authorized the fish bounty in 1789, it legislated that cod fishermen work on a share system by which "the fish, or proceeds of such fishing voyage or voyages...shall be divided among [the fishermen], in proportion to the quantities or number of said fish they may respectively have caught." This law was simply a codification of a fundamentally democratic practice that prevailed in the fisheries since the colonial period. The value of the crew's share differed from place to place—three-quarters, five-eighths, a half—but for the most part fishermen contributed the same share of the expenses of running the boat as they received of the profits. With the repeal of the law, captains and owners were free to pay their crew fixed salaries, as was the case in other fisheries. Although the change from shares to wages was neither immediate nor universal, in an age when there was no minimum wage, this changed the relationship between captain or owner and his crew. (Today, most trawlers work on a share basis, with a 60-to-40 split between the boat and the crew, who number about six. The higher share for the boat reflects the high costs of gear, fuel, provisions, and general maintenance.) Those fishermen who could not afford to buy their own boats and gear were forced to become employees of those who could, and the majority of the richer schooner owners, or groups of owners, lived in the wealthier parts of the state along Casco Bay and in southern Maine.

Because Portland was the financial capital of Maine, within fifteen years of the repeal of the fish bounty, southern Maine's share of the fishing fleet jumped from one-third to two-thirds, and a quarter of Maine's fishing fleet was based in Portland. Capital was not the only reason for the dramatic realignment of the Maine fishing industry. Starting in the 1840s, people of means began to express a marked preference for fresh fish over cured fish. The rise of the ice industry made it possible to preserve fish long enough to reach the table even in warm climates, but speed was still essential. The fresh-fish market depended almost entirely on fishermen's access to railroads, and Portland was the easternmost fishing community with train service until after the Civil War. The railroad reached Rockland on the southwest coast of Penobscot Bay in 1872, Mount Desert in 1884, and coastal Washington County only in 1899.

Without access to the fresh-fish market, the fishermen of eastern Maine had to rely on salt cod and smoked herring, but in this they were undercut by rivalry from Canada's neighboring Maritime Provinces. Cheaper labor, gear, and vessels, proximity to the fishing grounds, growing population, better access to the West Indian markets, and, in 1882, passage of a Canadian fishing bounty law were all factors in the rapid rise of the Nova

Scotia fisheries after the American Civil War. The enormous pressures on what had been a pillar of the Down East economy from Canada and Massachusetts, combined with the attraction of the recently tamed American West, had drastic implications for the fishing communities of eastern Maine, two-thirds of which suffered declines in population between 1860 and 1880.

Unable to compete in the deep-sea cod fisheries, those fishermen who remained worked the shore fisheries, principally for herring, mackerel, and lobsters. Unlike cod and haddock, mack-

N. C. Wyeth's *Dark Harbor Fishermen* (1943) seem to have little time for anything but fish. The granddaughter of Fernie Dell Barton (seated) and Fred Otis Dodge (standing with basket) also identified Franker Dyer ("the man knitting the fish") and Carl Pike (left).
COURTESY PORTLAND MUSEUM OF ART, PORTLAND

erel are pelagic fish found near the surface of the sea. There are a variety of ways to catch mackerel, the most common being with a purse seine net, which was introduced into the Maine fisheries in the 1860s. Modern seine nets are as large as seventy feet deep and 1,200 feet long—though they can run much longer. The top is kept on the surface by a line of floats, while a weighted line is suspended from the bottom of the net. Once a seiner locates a school of mackerel or herring, a smaller seine boat pays out the net to encircle the fish. Two purse lines leading to the bottom of the net are then hauled in to draw the net closed from the bottom. The fish are then brailed out of the seine; the brail nets of the nineteenth century gave way to pumps which vacuum the catch directly into the hold of the seiner. Although it is an efficient way of catching fish—especially with the development of advanced sonar systems that enable fishermen to see below the surface of the water—seine fishing is labor- and capital-intensive.

Herring, even more abundant in the Gulf of Maine than mackerel, is also caught by seining as well as in fish weirs, the latter being used especially east of Penobscot Bay. The family *clupeidae* includes not only herring *(Clupea harengus)*, the smallest of which are canned as sardines, but also sprats and alewives, which are found in freshwater habitats. They can be caught by midwater trawling, purse seining, gillnetting, and in fish weirs, and they can be smoked, pickled, salted, and canned, or fresh frozen.

Introduced from Norway in the 1880s, gillnetting is a type of net fishing that is much cheaper than either the seine net or otter trawl. Like a seine net, the gillnet hangs from the surface of the water like an underwater tennis net, but it is anchored in place rather than drawn closed. The mesh in a gillnet is sized so that only the head of a fish can fit. When the fish attempts to back out, its gills catch on the net and it drowns. One reason that it is so inexpensive to fish with anchored gillnets or free-floating drift nets is that both can be left untended. Environmentalists and others object to the use of gillnets because they are not

The Maine Child Labor Law of 1887 prohibited children under twelve from working in manufacturing or mechanical establishments, except for canneries. Cutters employed by the sardine factory were usually eight to fifteen years old. COURTESY MAINE MARITIME MUSEUM, BATH

species-specific and if the buoy markers are lost or the nets break free of their moorings they become "ghost fishers" that continue to catch fish that are never harvested.

Eventually one of the cornerstones of the herring market came to be the sardine, a type of canned herring, and from about 1875 canneries were a major employer in many Down East communities, especially around Machias and Passamaquoddy Bay. The first cannery opened in 1875, and the industry grew spectacularly. Within eleven years, the canneries alone employed more than 4,100 workers, and there were another 1,300 weir fishermen and boatmen, the majority of them concentrated around Lubec and Eastport. (Today the combined population of Lubec and Eastport is less than 4,000.) Sardines were caught almost entirely in fish weirs built in shoal waters along the coast. The industry's great appeal lay in its profitability, and the fact that entry into the industry was affordable. The costs of both a weir and a boat from which to tend it seldom cost more than $1,000 total, and the more successful fishermen could gross ten times that in a single year. After the 1950s the Maine herring canneries went into a decline, and by the 1990s only a few canneries remained. Herring remained commercially viable, but at the end of the twentieth century, the majority of the herring caught in the Maine fishery was used as bait fish exported to the West and Gulf Coast crab fisheries, and within Maine for lobster bait.

Through one of the curious evolutions to which the Maine seafood fisheries are prone the first fish to become commercially viable thanks to canning was lobster. In the two hundred years after European settlement, lobsters were caught only for local consumption and also for use as fertilizer on saltwater farms. The first settlers recorded catching lobsters by hand at the water's edge. Eventually lobsters could no longer be found right at the shore and they were caught in fyke or hoop nets left on the sea bottom until a lobster walked over it to take the bait.

Lobsters remained an item for local consumption only until the 1820s when fish merchants from southern New England began coming to Maine for lobsters. (Smacks were vessels designed to carry live fish to market.) Lobster smacks incorporated special pens amidships with holes drilled through the planking to admit seawater. These tanks made it possible to keep the lobsters alive until they reached the cannery or a market, usually in Boston or Portland. Canneries appeared on the Maine coast in the 1840s and had an almost immediate impact on the fishing industry. Initially a shore fishery carried out from dories and skiffs, lobstermen were rapidly forced to move farther offshore in pursuit of their prey.

By the 1870s the first boats tailor-made for the fishery appeared in Penobscot Bay. Measuring 15 to 20 feet in length, the shallow-draft, double-ended peapod was rowed by an oarsman who stood facing forward. The heavily built peapods were ideal for work in the shallow clefts of rocky ledges favored by lobsters, as well as in deeper water. The 1880s also saw the development of the gaff-rigged Maine fishing sloop or sloop boat, built on Muscongus Bay near the most productive lobstering grounds on the coast. With sharp, clipper-like lines, they measured anywhere from 16 to 40 feet in length, not including a long bowsprit and overhanging boom astern. Today these are best known through surviving models as the fixed-keel Friendship sloop and the centerboard Muscongus Bay sloop.

The lobster fishery had two distinct markets, the canneries and the restaurant market. The latter required a whole lobster of at least one pound for presentation purposes. Since canneries used only cooked meat, the size of the lobsters from which the meat came made no difference. As fishermen intensified their efforts and sold whatever they caught regardless of the lobsters' size or reproductive capacity, people grew concerned about the viability of the fishery. The first lobster laws, dating from the 1870s, prohibited the taking of egg-bearing lobsters, closed the fishery at certain times of year, and established a minimum size for taking

A smorgasbord of 180 years of lobster boats on the Maine coast.
DRAWING BY DOUGLAS ALVORD, COURTESY MAINE MARITIME MUSEUM, BATH

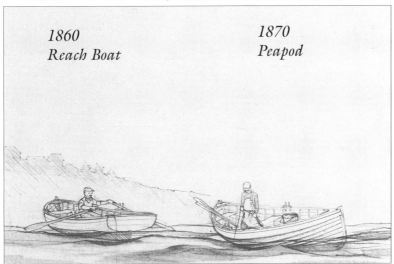

1860
Reach Boat

1870
Peapod

lobsters of 10.5 inches. The lobster laws have changed almost decade by decade to reflect new understanding of, or opinions
about, the state of lobster markets, the industry, the impact of
technology, and scientific knowledge. The adoption of a firm,
year-round minimum size law in 1895 ended the canning of lobster in Maine, although the live market continued.

By the end of the 1880s, there were about 2,000 lobstermen
in Maine and the annual catch averaged about 25 million pounds.
The turn of the century saw the development of the lobster
pound, a segregated part of a cove where lobsters could be maintained in a natural environment until the market price favored
the fishermen or, if the lobsters were caught as shedders, that is
when they were molting, they could be kept until their shells
hardened. The year 1903 saw the introduction of engines to
boats in the lobster fishery. Once they became available, small
"one-lunger" or "make-and-break" engines were almost univer-

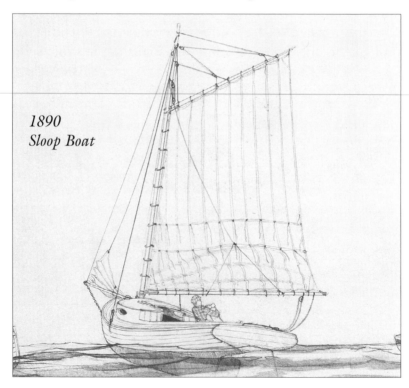

1890
Sloop Boat

sally embraced by lobstermen the length of the coast. Engines made fishing safer, extended the range over which one could fish, and their operation required less physical labor. Fishermen no longer had to row or sail their boats to where their traps were set, and they could also adapt their engines to power a mechanical winch with which to haul the lobster pots up from the bottom. Taken together these advantages made it possible for fishermen to set many more traps than ever before. In hindsight, the results seem predictable.

After averaging about 24 million pounds per year at the turn of the century, in 1913 the lobster catch plummeted to only 6 million pounds. The fishery recovered somewhat by the end of World War I, but by the 1930s it was again in decline. There was little market for fresh lobster because of the Depression, but for reasons not well understood there does not seem to have been a corresponding increase in lobster populations. The latest resurgence of the fishery began in the 1980s, and by the end of the century lobstering was the most recognizable fishery in the state. More than 140 coastal and island communities from Kittery to Eastport had a lobster fleet of some size and approximately

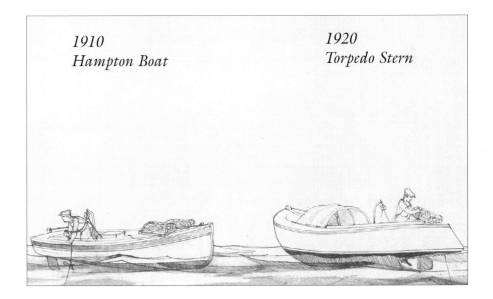

1910
Hampton Boat

1920
Torpedo Stern

7,000 people set 2.5 million traps to catch some 40 million pounds of lobster annually. Despite the intensive fishing, neither science nor fishermen can adequately explain how, or for how long, the lobster fishery can sustain itself. As Maine's commercial fisheries have been prone to periodic cycles of boom and bust over the past two centuries, concern about the sustainability of any segment of the fishing industry is always nagging just below the surface of prosperity.

Apart from the silhouette of the lobster itself, the most readily identifiable icon of the modern fishery is the lobster boat from which lobstermen set and haul their traps. To the untrained eye, most lobster boats look alike in profile, with a high, sharp bow, raised cabin and wheelhouse amidships, and a low-slung stern. With its relative simplicity of line, the lobster boat is a masterpiece of utilitarian elegance, and its evolution is a subject of endless fascination to boatbuilders and historians of boat design. Lobster boats of the early 2000s tend to derive from one of two earlier engine-less vessels. The so-called Hampton boat was first built in Hampton, on New Hampshire's 19-mile-long seacoast. Originally a double-ended boat, Maine builders apparently

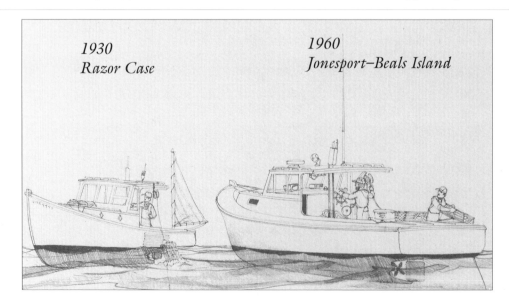

1930
Razor Case

1960
Jonesport–Beals Island

modified the basic hull form by giving the stern a flat transom, which made it well adapted to take an engine. Similar to but somewhat narrower than the Hampton boat was the Reach boat, so named for Moosabec or Eggemoggin Reach, east of Penobscot Bay, where the boat originated. In the first two decades of the 1900s, the modified Reach boat emerged as the Jonesport or Beals lobster boat. With a length-to-beam ratio of 4:1, the Jonesporter tends to have finer lines than the lobster boats of western Maine, and they generally prove faster in the annual lobster boat races held up and down the coast each summer.

The uncertainty that surrounds the lobster fishery stems in large part from an awareness of the fate of the other fisheries. There are only a handful of canneries left in the state, but most ominous is the demise of the cod and other commercial species. In 1934 a state report on the status of the fisheries stated plainly that it was "an established fact that most species of groundfish are growing scarcer in our bays, harbors, and inlets." But stocks began to decline precipitously in the 1960s, when hundreds of foreign fishing vessels began to fish the Gulf of Maine. In the space of a few years, landings of the three major species collapsed, one after the other. Between about 1960 and 1965, the haddock catch more than tripled to 150 million pounds, and then fell. Annual cod landings plummeted from 50 million pounds to 13 million pounds. Herring landings, too, declined.

In 1976 the U.S. Congress passed the Magnuson Fishery Conservation and Management Act under which foreign fishing vessels were prohibited from fishing within a 200-mile (322-kilometer) Exclusive Economic Zone, or EEZ. Passage of the law probably owed as much to the political climate of the time as it did to a comprehensive search for sound fishing policy; the majority of foreign vessels operating in the Gulf of Maine were from Eastern European countries dominated by the Soviet Union. In the absence of such fierce, subsidized competition, U.S. fishing vessels flocked back to the fisheries. But even as the num-

Chenoweth Hall's whimsical *Fishermen at Petit Point Manan* (1936).
COURTESY BATES COLLEGE MUSEUM OF ART, LEWISTON

ber of fishing vessels on the Banks rose 60 percent, to more than 1,000 in 1984, the total catch was falling drastically. Attempts to establish cod quotas were unavailing, and in 1996 Canada completely shut down its cod fishery. At the same time, the U.S. government began to tighten quotas on catch, to close specific areas to fishing, and to implement a boat buy-back program to help fishermen get out of the business and relieve pressure on the depleted fish stocks. Ten or fifteen years before, the government had subsidized the purchase of many of the same boats in an effort to help fishermen eager to exploit the new opportunities presented by the departure of the foreign fleets.

Whether these measures will result in a renewal of traditional deep-sea fish stocks is an unknown. Also unknown is what measures will or can be taken in the future to assure that the fisheries can be sustained over the long term. In the meantime, the Maine fisheries appear to be on the threshold of a new phase of development centered on aquaculture, the raising and

This period photo shows a clam digger bending to his work with a clam rake. Long closed because of pollution, several major clam flats around Maine have recently reopened.
COURTESY MAINE HISTORICAL SOCIETY, PORTLAND

harvesting of fish stocks previously found only in the wild. This fledgling industry began with a series of attempts to develop salmon and trout pens in the 1970s, but was hampered by insufficient capital, a lack of experience, and, in 1976 and 1981, unseasonably cold weather that killed a majority of the stocks. There were significant improvements in the 1980s, and by the end of the 1990s, eighteen Maine aquaculture companies were harvesting approximately 14 million pounds of salmon annually. The farming of mussels, oysters, and some varieties of seaweed—especially *nori* used in wrapping sushi—has also expanded considerably. The greatest threats to Maine aquaculture come from the uncertain economics of the industry, which requires fixed long-term capital expenditures in a market prone to dramatic price fluctuations, competition from imported fish, and a variety of environmental issues.

ELEVEN

Diversification

BY THE SECOND half of the nineteenth century, coastal communities from Kittery to Calais were starting to accommodate a new seasonal economy based less on the migration of fish and the harvest of crops and more on summer residents and tourism. The start of the latter industry cannot be fixed with any precision, but it certainly owed something to the published musings on the natural beauty of Maine by such authors as Harriet Beecher Stowe, who lived in Brunswick from 1850 to 1852. Stowe was particularly taken by the juxtaposition of Maine's closed and unadorned forest with the changeable vitality of her seas. She wrote,

> YOU ARE RIDING along in a lonely road, by some bay that seems to you like a secluded inland lake; you check your horse, to notice the fine outline of the various points, when lo! from behind one of them, swan-like, with wings all spread, glides in a ship from India or China, and wakes up the silence, by tumbling her great anchor into the water... and that ship connects these piney hills and rocky shores,

these spruces and firs, with distant lands of palm and spice, and speaks to you, in these solitudes, of groves of citron and olive.

In fact, there was little direct commerce between Maine and oriental ports, but Maine merchants and shipbuilders were actively involved in Asian trade. Among the earliest published reflections on the essential beauty of Maine, Stowe's essay ran in the *National Era* (which was publishing her *Uncle Tom's Cabin* in serial form). At the same time, American painters were also capturing on canvas the majesty of the Maine coast.

Starting in the 1830s, the area around Mount Desert attracted a growing number of American visual artists drawn by reports of "scenery so grand and beautiful as to be unsurpassed by any on the whole American coast." So wrote Francis Stevens of Castine, describing an 1850 visit to Mount Desert with his friend Fitz Hugh Lane. "The beauties of this place is [sic] well known and

Emily Lansingh Muir's watercolor, *Frieze #2* (1960s) illustrates "the fine outline of the various points" along the coast about which Harriet Beecher Stowe wrote a century before.
Courtesy University of Maine Museum of Art, Orono

John Marin, *Cape Split, Maine: Seashore and Trees* (1936).
COURTESY OGUNQUIT MUSEUM OF ART, OGUNQUIT

appreciated among artists…. But how unsatisfying a few days to an artist, when many months' sketching would scarcely suffice amid such exhaustless wealth of scenery." Among the other painters who happened to be on Mount Desert at the same time were Benjamin Champney, John Frederick Kensett, and Frederic Edwin Church—all of them practitioners of a romantic style that sought to announce their personal affinity with nature in the face of the rapid industrialization of America. In the work of these mid-century American artists, people and their creations—whether ships or lighthouses or buildings—exist in the shadow of a nature variously threatening or serene. The seascape continues to absorb, and writing from the vantage of a completely different artistic tradition eighty years after Lane, the modernist John Marin could still write of his adopted home on Cape Split, "Here the sea is so damned insistent that houses and land things won't appear much in my pictures."

Bar Harbor in its heyday; the passenger steamer *Mount Desert*
served on Penobscot Bay from 1879 to 1904.
COURTESY MAINE HISTORICAL SOCIETY, PORTLAND

What is interesting about artists associated with the Maine
coast is that while many are identified with particular schools or
styles of painting—the Hudson River school in the case of Church
and luminism in that of Lane, for instance—Maine itself was not
identified with any particular style. It had a universal appeal both
for artists who sought to render the coast on canvas, or for those
who simply wanted a place to visit and reflect. An unintended
consequence of these artistic celebrations was the promotion of
Maine to ever-larger numbers of visitors who "even the prosaic
folk, go prepared to enjoy the picturesque, the beautiful, the
sublime." Tourism in a variety of forms was beginning to assume
a significant role in the life of both coastal and inland Maine.

Mount Desert's Bar Harbor—then named Eden—was one of
the first communities to become a summer destination. After the
Civil War the number of hotels grew rapidly. At the height of the
season in 1880 the town was host to some 5,000 "rusticators,"

Pleasure boating on the Kennebunk at the turn of the century.

most of them young and well-to-do. In that decade, the town experienced a building boom as railroad barons, lottery kings, politicians, philanthropists, and scions of the Gilded Age threw up an imaginative assortment of "cottages" with architectural styles that ran the gamut from Italianate villas like "Buonriposo" to eccentric piles like "The Craigs," which an architectural historian described as "a kind of fantastic feudal castle, a hodgepodge of picturesque bits and romantic skylines, an exacerbation of the industrialist's dream of the picturesque." The locals' seasonal devotion to visitors was so pronounced that in the autumn of 1884, the *Mount Desert Herald* quoted the prayer of a local church elder: "Oh, Lord, now that our summer visitors have departed, wilt Thou take their places in our hearts." This droll assessment of the economic role of tourism gradually gave way to a tendency to regard people from out-of-state as alien. Visitors were viewed with a guarded reserve and described as people "from away," even if they chose to put down roots.

In the early twentieth century, Bar Harbor became a warm-weather sanctuary for Washington officials and the Navy established a coaling station at Lamoine on the mainland to serve President Theodore Roosevelt's Great White Fleet, which visited Bar Harbor, as did major ocean liners of the day. (Bar Harbor remains a popular cruise ship destination, and both Bar Harbor and Portland offer daily steamship service to Yarmouth, Nova Scotia, in all but the winter months.) The summer bustle resulted in the creation of satellite communities around Frenchman Bay and connected to one another by steamer ferries. By the 1920s Hancock Point had 10,000 summer visitors and 100 restaurants to accommodate them.

Summer people were not restricted to Mount Desert and environs. Providing room and board for guests was a fairly simple matter and resort communities blossomed along the coast, especially in the south. Old Orchard Beach originally attracted bathers from neighboring Biddeford and Saco. The construction of boardinghouses, camps, and inns led to an influx of French-Canadians who traveled overland from Quebec to spend summers by the sea. More fashionable still were Kennebunk and Kennebunkport, whose reputations were considerably enhanced in the 1980s when President George H. W. Bush's family home at Walker's Point became the site of the summer White House.

Before World War I Bar Harbor's concentration of wealth and political influence had made it a discreet cornucopia for Portland resident and Navy commander, Robert E. Peary, who needed money and government approval for an Arctic exploration vessel. He received both and commissioned a Bucksport shipyard to build a vessel suitable for Arctic exploration. Aptly named for President Theodore Roosevelt, whose administration Perry lobbied vigorously, the *Roosevelt* was launched in 1905 from the McKay and Dix Shipyard on Verona Island, Bucksport. An auxiliary-powered three-masted schooner, this was the first U.S.-flag vessel designed and built expressly for Arctic research. Having obtained a leave from the Navy, Commander Peary sailed the *Roosevelt* to New York for fitting out and a gala departure on the second of his three attempts to reach the North Pole.

The *Roosevelt*'s master on this voyage was Donald B. Mac-Millan, a veteran of several polar expeditions and, subsequently, a four-year stint in Greenland among other northern expeditions. After World War I MacMillan ordered the two-masted wooden polar schooner from Hodgdon Brothers in East Boothbay. Named for MacMillan's alma mater, *Bowdoin* was stoutly built, with a steel-sheathed bow, simple pole masts, and no bowsprit. On July 6, 1921, she departed Wiscasset on the first of twenty-six voyages north under "Mac." Sponsored by the Carnegie Foundation and planned for a study of terrestrial magnetism and atmospheric electricity, this first voyage took *Bowdoin* into Hudson Strait to Schooner Harbor on Foxe Peninsula.

Sponsors of subsequent expeditions, to study radio communications, meteorological phenomena, Arctic flora and fauna,

The schooner *Bowdoin*, sailing in her element again.
COURTESY MAINE MARITIME ACADEMY, CASTINE

and perform hydrographic surveys, included the U.S. Navy and the National Geographic Society. In 1930 *Bowdoin* carried students for the first time, and from 1934 on she always sailed with students who paid for the privilege of sailing with "Mac" to the high north. Despite his previous insistence that no woman would (or could) sail to the Arctic, in 1938 his wife, Miriam, accompanied him to Greenland. (In all, "Lady Mac" would make nine voyages with her husband aboard *Bowdoin*. Her glowing accounts of the voyages tended to gloss over the hardships, and veterans of the northern voyages referred to her memoir *Green Seas and White Ice* as "Green Seas and White Lies.")

After two wartime survey voyages to Greenland, *Bowdoin* was laid up until 1946. MacMillan made his last voyage in her in 1954, at the age of eighty, and she was sold to Mystic Seaport Museum. She returned to Maine waters nine years later, and after a stint as a charter boat, she underwent a lengthy rebuild before joining the fleet of the Maine Maritime Academy at Castine in 1989. The State of Maine's official sail-training ship, she visited Labrador for the first time in a quarter century in 1990. In the meantime, Bowdoin College opened the Peary-MacMillan Arctic Museum in Brunswick. Admiral Peary's summer house on Eagle Island is also part of the Eagle Island State Historic Site.

By the time Peary ordered the *Roosevelt* from McKay and Dix, Bucksport was past its prime, but the growing summer trade brought a demand for racing class boats—vessels of the same design and same sail area—a demand the port's remaining shipyards could easily satisfy. Around the turn of the century the editor of *The Rudder* magazine, Thomas Fleming Day, advanced a radical theory of pleasure sailing. "The danger of the sea for generations has been preached by the ignorant," wrote Day. "Small vessels are safer than large, providing they are properly designed, strongly built, thoroughly equipped, and skillfully manned." The backbone of good seamanship is "confidence in yourself, confidence in your craft, confidence in your crew." Coupled with changes in work habits and new ideas about leisure time, Day's philosophy had a profound effect on the status and nature of boating for pleasure.

The new interest in amateur sailing could not have found more fertile ground than the coast of Maine, which boasted a diversity of practical boat types and a large number of skilled boatbuilders. Naval architects and designers such as Edward and W. Starling Burgess and John Alden drew whole fleets of handy racing and cruising boats, including the Winter Harbor 21, the Mount Desert A boat, the Dark Harbor 17, the Christmas Cove 21, and the North Haven dinghy, dating from the 1880s and the oldest one-design racing class in the country. The advent of the gasoline engine rendered a number of once common fishing vessels such as the peapod and dory obsolete, but they and others proved easily adapted to the needs of recreational boaters. The Friendship sloop proved an excellent cruiser, although the traditional lofty rig was often reduced somewhat in the interest of easier handling.

Although it is known today chiefly for its warships, Bath Iron Works probably did as much as any single shipyard to establish Maine's reputation for yacht construction. By the end of the nineteenth century, the American public was fascinated with yachting, especially the *America's* Cup races, in large part because the people involved were well-known leaders of American business and society whose every move afloat or ashore was fodder for the daily press. Maine's long association with the international race series dates from at least 1886, when Deer Isle fishermen comprised half the crew of the Cup defender *Mayflower*, and the next year they made up half the crew of *Volunteer*. In 1895, in the waters off New York Harbor, an all-Deer Isle crew sailed *Defender* to victory over the English challenger *Valkyrie III*. The only non-Mainer in *Columbia's* crew in 1899—against the first of Sir Arthur Lipton's five unsuccessful challenges, in *Shamrock*—was the brilliant Scottish helmsman Charles Barr.

The first Maine-built *America's* Cup defender was the Hodgdon Brothers' *Defiance,* launched at East Boothbay in 1914.

The primary contractor for the job was Bath Iron Works, which subcontracted the decking, planking, and caulking to Hodgdon Brothers. World War I brought a temporary end to *America's* Cup competition and *Defiance* was scrapped in 1915. The succession of yachts that comprised a good part of Bath Iron Works business before World War II included J. P. Morgan II's turbo-electric-powered *Corsair IV*, launched in 1930. With a length of 343 feet, it was the largest private yacht built in the United States. *Corsair IV* paid annual visits to Islesboro in Penobscot Bay, although the ship reportedly attracted more curiosity than Morgan could endure. In his fondness for yachts, J. P. Morgan II was following in the wake of his financier father, an enthusiastic yachtsman who served as Commodore of the New York Yacht Club and had a long involvement with the *America's* Cup races.

At 343.5 feet, J. P. Morgan, Jr.'s *Corsair IV* was the largest private yacht built in the United States. COURTESY MAINE MARITIME MUSEUM, BATH

The triumvirate responsible for the unrivalled *America*'s
Cup defender *Ranger*, from left to right: Olin Stephens,
Harold Vanderbilt, and W. Starling Burgess.

In 1937 at the height of the Great Depression, Bath Iron
Works launched the J-Class sloop *Ranger* for Harold S. Vanderbilt, who was mounting a defense against T. O. M. Sopwith's
America's Cup challenger *Endeavour II*. (Sopwith was the British airplane manufacturer responsible for the fighter biplane of
World War I and "Peanuts" comic strip fame.) *Ranger* was the
last J-boat to defend the Cup and her unparalleled performance
resulted in national public recognition for Bath Iron Works.
Among the fastest and most beautiful Cup defenders ever, *Ranger*
was designed by W. Starling Burgess and Olin J. Stephens II. As
an anonymous observer wrote:

> W. STARLING BURGESS and Olin J. Stephens, in designing
> *Ranger*, hit on something that jumped over some twenty
> years of normal progress in yacht design and came down
> with a boat whose speed, compared with her contempo-
> raries, was nothing short of phenomenal.

Burgess, who had a reputation for speed, had moved his office to Bath in 1935 to work on designs for a revolutionary destroyer with an aluminum-alloy hull and said to be capable of speeds of 52 knots. He brought a wealth of experience to his work, having previously designed the Cup defenders *Enterprise* and *Rainbow*, as well as the largest five-masted schooner ever built, the *Jane Palmer*, one of the few five-masters built outside of Maine. He was also noted for his fast fishing schooners, which contemporaries described as yachts in disguise. Stephens, who at age twenty-three had designed the yawl *Dorade* and then sailed her to victory in the 1931 Transatlantic and Fastnet races, was relief helmsman in *Ranger*.

Money was scarce and Vanderbilt was unable to form a syndicate for the Cup defense, but BIW president Pete Newell agreed to build *Ranger* at a reduced cost. During her career, which was ended by the approach of World War II, *Ranger* finished 34 races of the 37 she entered. *Ranger* won 32 of those 34 races. The two losses were wind-searching, drifting matches which her opponents won by only 45 seconds. Her average winning time overall was 7 minutes, 42 seconds, and in her four-race sweep against *Endeavour II,* her average lead was 10 minutes, 55 seconds— large margins in sailboat racing. In 1941 *Ranger* was broken up for scrap, and Bath Iron Works began accelerating its destroyer-building program for the Navy.

As a partner in Sparkman and Stephens, Olin Stephens went on to draw scores of yachts whose designs are replicated today in vessels produced by The Hinckley Company in Southwest Harbor on Mount Desert Island. Maine's association with the *America's* Cup was renewed in the 1980s and 1990s when executives from Hinckley and AeroHydro, also based in Southwest Harbor, were part of the syndicate behind *Stars and Stripes* in its 1987 challenge to *Kookaburra II*. AeroHydro also led the design effort for the multi-hulled Cup defender *Stars and Stripes* in 1988, and in 1995 its technology was used by Team New Zealand to

No contest: The four-masted schooner *Herbert L. Rawding*,
built at Stockton Springs in 1919, and the J-class *Ranger*, built
at Bath in 1937. COURTESY OF THE ROSENFELD COLLECTION,
MYSTIC SEAPORT MUSEUM, INC., MYSTIC, CONNECTICUT

develop their successful challenger *Black Magic*. In 2000 the
South Portland-based *Young America* syndicate was the favored
challenger to New Zealand, but its hopes were dashed when the
hull of *USA 53* broke in half and nearly sank during an early
challenge match.

Despite its outstanding reputation for a handful of celebrated yachts, and a few post-World War II building programs involving trawlers, tankers, and other merchant vessels, in the last half of the twentieth century Bath Iron Works was known chiefly for its naval construction. Bath Iron Works built thirteen destroyers in the late 1930s and although work on Burgess's experimental aluminum destroyer was eventually dropped, between June 1940 and January 1945 a total of eighty-three destroyers were ordered from BIW. This was a quarter of all the destroyers built in the United States in the same period, and more than were built by all Japanese shipyards combined. Two of particular note are the *Sumner*-class USS *Laffey* and USS *Maddox*. In April 1945 the *Laffey* earned the epithet "The ship that would not die" after being hit by five kamikazes and bombs from eight more in an hour-long engagement off Okinawa. She is now a museum ship at Patriots Point Maritime Museum in Mt. Pleasant, South Carolina. The *Maddox* was also on station off Okinawa, but she is best known for her operations off Vietnam in August 1964. Her

"The ship that would not die," USS *Laffey* (DD–724) seen here before her titanic struggle against waves of kamikazes off Okinawa on April 16, 1945. Courtesy Maine Maritime Museum, Bath

engagement with North Vietnamese gunboats led to Congressional passage of President Lyndon Johnson's Gulf of Tonkin Resolution, which committed the United States to nearly nine years of undeclared war in Vietnam.

At the U.S. Navy yard in Kittery, submarine production also accelerated before the United States entered World War II, and Kittery turned out another seventy-five fleet submarines—more than a quarter of all U.S. submarines built between 1940 and 1945. Although less heralded than the German U-boat campaign in the Battle of the Atlantic, the U.S. Navy's submarine offensive against Japan's merchant fleet crippled the Japanese military machine by cutting off its vital oil supplies from Indonesia. Overall submarines accounted for 60 percent of all Japanese merchant ships sunk, and 30 percent of all Japanese warships.

Sadly, among the better-known submarines launched into the Piscataqua were the USS *Squalus* and *Sculpin*, a pair linked in tragedy. Commissioned on March 1, 1939, *Squalus* was on a test run thirteen miles southeast of Kittery on May 23 when the main induction valve leading to the engine room failed. Twenty-three of her men drowned before the bulkhead door to the engine room was secured and thirty-three crew members remained alive in the forward part of the hull, which lay in about 240 feet of water. The stricken submarine was discovered by her sister ship USS *Sculpin*, and with the assistance of the submarine rescue ship USS *Falcon*, her survivors were brought safely to the surface with a McCann diving bell. Three months later the hull was raised, and after an extensive refit she was recommissioned as USS *Sailfish* and dispatched to the Pacific. On the night of December 3, 1943, she sank the light carrier *Chuyo* about 250 miles southeast of Tokyo. Among the hundreds of men lost with the Japanese ship were twenty prisoners of war from the *Sculpin*, which had been sunk in the Caroline Islands two weeks before.

Kittery remained an important shipyard well into the Cold War. The most important submarine launched there after World War II was the USS *Albacore* (1953), specifically designed to help the Navy develop a hull of optimal hydrodynamic efficiency that could also accommodate a nuclear reactor. *Albacore's* hull shape was revolutionary, the most obvious difference from her predecessors being the rounded surfaces of the hull and the abandonment of deck guns and other fittings that impede hydrodynamic efficiency, a concept that has since become universal. Submarines of World War II vintage, by contrast, looked like narrow boats with pointed bows and flat decks. Although *Albacore* was driven by diesel-electric propulsion, nuclear power plants were just over the horizon, and the world's first nuclear submarine, the Connecticut-built USS *Nautilus*, was commissioned in 1955.

As important as their contributions to the Allied effort were in terms of destroyers, submarines, and other naval vessels, Maine shipyards also played a crucial role in the construction of merchant ships during World War II. In April 1941 Bath Iron Works collaborated with Todd Shipyard of Philadelphia to form what became the South Portland Shipbuilding Corporation. This shipyard was established to build Ocean Class freighters for the British government, whose merchant fleet was being ravaged by German U-Boats. *Ocean Liberty* was the prototype, modeled on a World War I-era British design that had never been built. As the war progressed, the Ocean Class design was borrowed by the United States and reconfigured as the Liberty ship. By war's end, the South Portland complex had built 30 Ocean Class freighters and 274 Liberty ships, 10 percent of all the Liberties built at seventeen shipyards around the country, and "more than a good-sized commercial shipyard could expect to produce in three decades at operation." Ungainly ships, the Liberties measured just over 440 feet in length and had a capacity of about 11,000 tons, the equivalent of about 300 railroad freight cars. Manned by a crew of about 45 merchant seamen, the "Ugly Ducklings," as President Franklin D. Roosevelt dubbed them, plowed through the seas at a speed of about 11 knots. For all their ungainly lumbering, the Liberties formed a vital "bridge of ships" that carried much-needed fuel oil and war materiel to Europe.

The most famous and long-lived of the South Portland Liberties was the *Jeremiah O'Brien,* named for the "Machias Admiral" of Revolutionary War fame. The *O'Brien* survived the war, as well as the subsequent post-war scrapping of the nation's surplus merchant fleet, and today she is preserved in working condition in San Francisco, as a memorial to wartime merchant mariners and their ships. She last visited her South Portland birthplace in 1994 during a voyage to France for ceremonies on the occasion of the fiftieth anniversary of the D-Day invasion.

The location of the South Portland yards was ideal for the kind of assembly-line mass production that the Liberty program required. The angle of the granite slope dipping into Casco Bay allowed for the construction of enclosed basins that could be flooded for fast launching. The basins could also be partitioned,

South Portland shipyards during World War II.
COURTESY PORTLAND HARBOR MUSEUM, SOUTH PORTLAND

which allowed for several ships to be built at once, and launched either singly or together. As noted previously, smaller independent yards elsewhere on the Maine coast produced hundreds of minesweepers, patrol boats, and a variety of utility boats for the Navy and Army. For many yards, financially debilitated by the Great Depression, war production provided the capital for a new start in the post-war years when Maine finally began to recover from the collapse of its timber and shipping industries. Yet no peacetime program could hope to guarantee the employment generated by the World War II shipbuilding programs. At Bath Iron Works alone, the payroll grew fivefold, from 4,000 to 20,300, and nearly 3,000 of the new workers were women.

Maine's overall contribution to the war effort in terms of shipbuilding is enumerated in statistics published on June 14, 1945. In all, twenty-four Maine boat- and shipyards built 1,358 vessels of all kinds—everything from skiffs and lifeboats to Liberty ships, destroyers, and submarines—for the government. These included 585 vessels for the Navy, 494 for the Army, and 279 for the Maritime Commission.

By the end of the twentieth century, ship- and boatbuilding in Maine was advancing on a variety of fronts from military to fishing boats to yachts. (At this point in history, United States shipyards had all but ceased to build ships for foreign trade.) Even as boat- and shipbuilders embraced state-of-the-art materials, designs, and technologies—including cold-molding, honeycomb, composite layering, and epoxy techniques, and gas plasma welding for BIW's guided missile destroyers—Maine also became the nursery of a movement that sought to preserve and encourage the craft of building wooden boats, whatever their purpose.

This effort began to take shape around Jon Wilson's founding of *WoodenBoat* magazine in the early 1970s. Much is made of the almost mystical affinity that people have for wooden boats, but the magazine's appeal is not restricted to enthusiasts for whom a wooden boat "feels more 'alive'" than one of fiberglass or steel. In cultivating a variety of complementary interests in technology, craftsmanship, scientific design, and materials, *WoodenBoat* became a clearinghouse of information for designers and builders who understand that wood is not an esoteric and antiquated medium for construction, but one that will probably be around for a good time to come, and the use of which is as susceptible to improvement and refinement as that of any other material. In so doing, the magazine put the town of Brooklin (population 800) at the center of an international network that reaches more than 100,000 builders, designers, and buyers from Louisiana to Indonesia and Australia to Denmark.

WoodenBoat Publications also runs a series of one- and two-week boatbuilding courses during the summer at its campus on Eggemoggin Reach. Schools, technical colleges, and museums around the state offer similar programs. Some are designed for aspiring professionals. Others offer courses lasting from one to fourteen days and catering to people for whom "the beautiful, the sublime" art of boatbuilding is no less worthy of their leisure time than sailing must have seemed to many a century ago, when Thomas Fleming Day preached his radical vision of small boats and self-confidence.

CODA

A Sense of Place

To A greater extent than most
other states, Maine has a pronounced identity, one shaped by its
place in the world. That identity has undergone many transfor-
mations in the past four centuries. For the Abnaki, it was the place
of the dawn. For European colonists who settled here, it was a
paradise of fish and fur and timber. In the early years of the Republic, shipwrights availed themselves of the abundant resources
available for their craft, and merchants capitalized on their easy
access to the world. Even as the center of power in national affairs
slipped south and west, Maine merchants and seamen continued
to play a formative role in world trade. In an age when the nature of sea trades seems to have all but displaced the need for the
mariner, thanks to a combination of geography and the traditions
that that geography has fostered, Maine remains a nursery for
seamen and a laboratory for experiment in maritime enterprise.

In the town of Castine overlooking the Bagaduce there is a
store called The Four Flags, a name that alludes to the town's
occupation by French, English, Dutch, and American forces.

Thanks to the Maine Maritime Academy, Castine is now home to a student body that may represent the flags of more than twenty different countries in a given year. One of five maritime colleges in the United States, the Academy (founded in the midst of World War II), is one of the world's premier institutions for training merchant seamen.

Although the volume of maritime trade increased at a dizzying pace over the course of the twentieth century, changes in technology and increases in productivity have made the seaman almost invisible in the modern world. At the turn of the last century, an efficient schooner such as *Wyoming* had a tonnage-to-crew ratio of less than 300-to-1. By contrast, the container ship *President Truman* (61,875 grt, 21 crew) has a ratio of 2,946-to-1. Such vessels are designed as part of a freight network that depends on ships, trains, and trucks for its efficiency. Such a highly integrated intermodal system puts extraordinary demands on ships' officers, whose experience and training must combine elements of seamanship and vessel operations—two constants in the ever-changing world of the maritime industries—with engineering, business management, and logistics. Just as ships launched from Maine yards in the nineteenth century secured Maine's reputation for excellence in ports worldwide, graduates of the Maine Maritime Academy maintain the state's reputation as a center of maritime enterprise.

That Maine continues to nurture such vital participants in the infrastructure of global trade is due to the fact that its citizens remain part of a real and immediate maritime culture in daily contact with the sea. While there are significant communities dependent on the sea that survive in other states such as Massachusetts, to name one example, the majority of Americans have little opportunity to engage the sea. In concluding such a survey of four hundred years, especially on the cusp of a new century and millennium, one is tempted to predict what these factors suggest about the future of maritime Maine.

If present ambition is any guide, then the future is very bright.

In the past twenty years, the state government has focused on developing a three-port strategy for Maine concentrated on Portland, Searsport, and Eastport. As of this writing, Portland is rated the largest port in New England by volume of tonnage handled, much of this volume being accounted for by shipments of oil bound for Canada. (The Portland pipeline opened during World War II so that tankers from South America could avoid the threat of German U-boats in the Gulf of Maine and the Gulf of St. Lawrence.) The port's diversified facilities also accommodate containerized freight, bulk cargoes, sizeable fishing and lobster fleets, recreational boaters, and a growing passenger trade that includes seasonal service to Nova Scotia and port visits by cruise ships.

There is additional international passenger service between Bar Harbor and Yarmouth, and the mainland is connected to Maine's fourteen year-round island communities by a variety of private and public ferry services. The state hopes to complement this existing passenger network with a "marine highway" linking Portland, Rockland, Bar Harbor, and Eastport via high-speed ferries, and some entrepreneurs have expressed an interest in a commuter ferry along the Kennebec between Bath and Augusta. Although the ice trade is no longer viable, the river freezes regardless, and such a service will also have a limited season.

The three-port strategy has been of great consequence to eastern Maine. Twenty years ago, Eastport had no commercial port to speak of. Today it is the only export-oriented port in New England, thanks to its success in capturing a stream of goods previously shipped via New Brunswick and Nova Scotia. Some people feel that the port might also benefit from the development of so-called "post-Panamax" ships such as the *President Truman*, that is, vessels too large to fit through the locks of the Panama Canal. Now that this barrier has been broken, we can expect to see container ships whose draft exceeds that of most existing ports. In this regard, Eastport's advantage is that it is the deepest natural port on the East Coast, with a mean low water depth of 64 feet—without dredging—far deeper than most other dredged ports. In addition, it is also the closest port to Europe in the United States.

The coast of Maine has always been praised for its fine harbors. As early as 1605, James Rosier noted that

> ...BY OPINION of others of good judgment in our shippe, here are more good harbors for ships of all burthens, than England afford, and far more secure from all winds, and weathers, than any in England, Scotland, France, or Spaine.

Little has changed in four hundred years, and much the same might be said of the coast of Maine today. But experience shows that favorable geography has its limits. Despite its advantages, Eastport is far removed from a major interstate highway, and there are no direct rail links to the port—two crucial elements in the modern world of intermodal transportation. Yet even if the solution to these problems appears fairly straightforward—

John Byrne's photomosaic, *Harbormaster* (1999), captures the essence of Portland's working waterfront at the end of the twentieth century. Some things never change. COURTESY THE ARTIST.

and ports obviously require a healthy infrastructure to meet the needs of merchant shippers—infrastructure is not the only key to their success. Writing about port development in general, Maine Maritime Academy alumnus and shipping executive Henry Powers observed:

> THE LOCATION of the port facility for importing or exporting goods and services has a direct relationship not only to the geography of the land, i.e., deep water, but also to its density of population, which usually coincides with that of the production of those goods and services.

Were the future of maritime Maine to be determined solely by centuries of accumulated experience in a variety of maritime industries coupled to a favorable geography, the path to prosperity would be clear. In point of fact, the future of maritime Maine will probably be decided less by competing interests on the high seas or at the water's edge than by landed interests eager to defend their own vision of "the way life should be," regardless of the ultimate cost.

Maritime Maine Chronology

1492	Christopher Columbus crosses Atlantic
1494	Treaty of Tordesillas divides world into Portuguese and Spanish spheres of influence
1497	John Cabot sails from England to Newfoundland or Nova Scotia
1524	Giovanni da Verrazano first European to describe Maine coast
1602	Bartholomew Gosnold expedition to Maine coast
1603	Martin Pring expedition to Maine coast
1604	Samuel de Champlain winters on St. Croix River
1605	George Waymouth expedition in Muscongus Bay
1607	London Company establishes Jamestown Colony in Virginia
	Plymouth Company establishes Popham Colony on Kennebec; shallop *Virginia* built
1609	Henry Hudson on Penobscot Bay
1614–15	John Smith publishes *A Description of New England*
1620	*Mayflower* to Plymouth
1620s	Estimated 400 European fishing vessels active on Maine coast
1622	Maine fishing posts in regular contact with Plymouth, Massachusetts
1631	First sawmill on Piscataqua River
1632	Treaty of St. Germain sets eastern Maine border at Penobscot River
1634	First cargo of masts exported from Penobscot Bay to England
1642–51	English Civil Wars
1651	English Parliament institutes first Navigation Acts
1652–1820	Maine subject to Massachusetts
1654–70	Acadia under loose English control following capture of St. John, Port Royal, and Pentagoët
1666–70	Second Anglo-Dutch War
1670	Acadia reverts to French control
1674	Adrien Aernouts establishes New Holland
1675–78	King Philip's War; Mugg captures more than twenty fishing boats
1677	Massachusetts buys Gorges' family claim to lands west of the Kennebec
1685	Crown appoints first Surveyor of Pine and Timber
1689–97/99	King William's War/War of the League of Augsburg

1690	William Phipps captures Port Royal, Acadia
	Population of Maine 2,000
1695	HMS *Falkland* built at Kittery
1697	Treaty of Ryswick moves border to Kennebec River or to St. Croix River
1702–13	Queen Anne's War/War of the Spanish Succession
1703	French Canadians and Micmacs raid coast between Wells and Casco Bay
1710	Port Royal captured by English for the last time
	Nottingham Galley sinks off Boon Island
1713	French Acadia ceded to Britain as Nova Scotia by Treaty of Utrecht
1716	First written use of "schooner"
1717	Falmouth (Portland) incorporated
1721–27	Dummer's War ends Abnaki threat to coastal settlements
1729	Act reserves for the Royal Navy all pine trees not privately owned—regardless of size—from Nova Scotia to New Jersey
1733	First shipment of limestone from Thomaston to Boston
1743	Population of Maine 12,000
1744–48	King George's War/War of the Austrian Succession
1745	William Pepperell captures Louisbourg
1756–63	French and Indian War/Seven Year's War
1763	Machias founded
1774 July	Coercive Acts close port of Boston
1775–83	American Revolution
1775 Apr.	Battles of Lexington and Concord
1775 June	Battle of Machias: capture of HMS *Margaretta*
1775 Sept.	Arnold expedition against Quebec leaves Massachusetts
1775 Oct.	HMS *Canceaux* destroys Falmouth (Portland)
1776	Bangor founded as Kenduskeag Plantation
1777	John Paul Jones's *Ranger* launched at Kittery
1779 Aug.	Penobscot Expedition ends with loss of 39 vessels—entire fleet
1783	Orders in Council keep U.S. ships from trading with West Indies, but allow U.S. ships to enter British ports with American goods on essentially pre-Revolution terms
1784	General Court of Massachusetts hangs "representation of a cod-fish" in the house
1787	"not a ship owned" in Portland
1789	Treasury Department assumes control of lighthouses
	Creation of Revenue Marine Service
	Codfishing bounties introduced
1790	Portland Head Light opens

1791–93	New Meadows Canal between New Meadows and Kennebec Rivers
1793 Nov.	Orders in Council authorizes seizure of U.S. ships trading with France; repealed Apr. 1794
1794 Nov.	Jay's Treaty opens British West Indies to American ships
1798	U.S. Navigation Act
1800 June	Navy Department establishes first government shipyard at Kittery
1801	Pasha of Tripoli declares war on United States
1804–1806	British Orders in Council and Napoleonic decrees close European ports to American ships and subject them to arrest on high seas
1807	Portland Observatory completed; death of Edward Preble
1807 Dec.	Jefferson signs Embargo Act; repealed Mar. 1, 1809
1812–15	War of 1812
1813 Sept. 5	HMS *Boxer* vs. USS *Enterprise*
1814 July 11	British capture Eastport
1814 Aug.	British capture Machias
1814 Sept.	British capture Bangor and Castine
1817 Mar.	Act Concerning the Navigation of the United States
1819	Codfishing bounty law revised
1820	Maine achieves statehood
1820s	Granite industry develops
1820s	Ice industry develops
1830–70	Cumberland and Oxford Canal
1831	*Waterville* first successful steamer on Kennebec River
1832	Capital moved to Augusta
1835	Steamer *Royal Tar* burns in Penobscot Bay
1838–1921	Logging maintains Telos Cut between Telos and Webster Lakes
1840s	Maine shipbuilders begin importing wood from southern states
	Fresh fish market develops
1842	*Bangor* becomes first American vessel to cross Atlantic under steam alone
1844	*Amphitrite* first steamer on Moosehead Lake for lumber industry
1845–55	Decade of the clipper
1848	Shore Village becomes Rockland and separates from Thomaston
1849	Longfellow writes "The Building of a Ship"
	Britain repeals Navigation Acts
	Lock on Kennebunk River enables construction of large ships above falls

1849	California gold rush spurs clipper ship construction
1850-59	Bath launches 12 schooners and 199 square-riggers
1851	*Nightingale* built at South Eliot on the Piscataqua
	Snow Squall built in South Portland
	Australian gold rush
1853	*Red Jacket* built at Thomaston
	Bath launches 172,000 tons of shipping; Waldoboro 40,453; Portland, 17,549
1856	Grand Trunk establishes direct rail service between Portland and Montreal
1857	Financial panic sweeps country; many shipyards close
1859	Thirteen customs districts in Maine
1860	3,376 ships clear port of Bangor, most with lumber
1860–65	American Civil War
1863 June 23	Confederates seize revenue cutter *Caleb Cushing* in Portland
1863 July 28	*Snow Squall* evades Confederate raider *Tuscaloosa*
1863	Transcontinental railroad completed
1866	Fire ravages Portland
	Codfishing bounty law repealed
1871	Direct rail link opened between Quebec and St. John, New Brunswick, via Bangor
	Caleb Cushing negotiates settlement of *"Alabama* Claims"
	Schooner *Lewis R. French* built at Christmas Cove
1872	Railroad reaches Rockland
1874	*Ocean King*, four-masted bark, built at Kennebunk
1875	First fish cannery opens in Maine
	Bath launches 54 of 79 square-riggers built in the U.S.
1876	Direct rail link opens between Quebec and Halifax, via Bangor
1880s	Bath launches 255 schooners, 62 square-riggers
1880	Bar Harbor hosts 5,000 "rusticators" at height of season
	First four-masted schooner, *William L. White*, built at Bath
1882	Canadian government passes fish bounty law
1883	Chesapeake and Ohio Railroad completes coal rail link from West Virginia to Norfolk, Virginia
1884	*Bradford C. French*, largest three-masted schooner, built at Kennebunk
	Railroad reaches Mount Desert
1886	Eastport and Lubec Canneries and related industries employ more than 5,000 people
1888	First East Coast five-masted schooner, *Gov. Ames*, built at Waldoboro
	North Haven dinghy emerges as racing class

1889	Arthur Sewall brings Scottish-built steel-hulled *Kenilworth* under U.S. flag
1890–92	Sewall launches last four wooden square-riggers
1893	Bath Iron Works delivers first steel gunboats to U.S. Navy
1895	State adopts minimum-size law for lobster
1896	Bath Iron Works builds ironclad ram, *Katahdin*
1898 Nov.	Steamer *Portland* lost in the *Portland* Gale
1899	Railroad reaches coastal Washington County
1900	First six-masted schooner, *George W. Wells,* built at Camden
	Iron barges adapted for lime trade
1902	Seven-masted schooner *Thomas W. Lawson* built in Massachusetts
1905	Peary launches the *Roosevelt* at Bucksport
1909	Last six-masted schooner, *Wyoming,* built in Bath
1911	Fire ravages Bangor
1913	Single customs district created for Maine and New Hampshire
	Lobster catch plummets to 6 million pounds
1914	Bath Iron Works builds Moosehead Lake steamer *Katahdin*
1921	*Bowdoin* launched at East Boothbay
1930	Morgan's *Corsair IV* built by Bath Iron Works
1934	State reports decline in ground fisheries
1937	Bath Iron Works builds *America's* Cup defender *Ranger*
1939	USS *Squalus* sinks on trials off Kittery
1941	Maine Maritime Academy founded at Castine
	Oil pipeline to Montreal opens
1942–45	274 Liberty ships built in South Portland
1947	Fire ravages Bar Harbor
1953	USS *Albacore* launched at Portsmouth Navy Yard
1974	*WoodenBoat* magazine founded
1976	Congress passes Magnuson Act
1981	State of Maine opens port of Eastport and adopts three-port strategy with Searsport and Portland
1989–94	Rise and fall of sea urchin fishery
1996	Canada closes cod fishery
1997	Governor King announces "Jobs from the Sea" to coordinate work of marine research institutions
1999	Lobster catch exceeds 40 million pounds
	Portland becomes largest port in New England in volume of cargo handled

Notes

6   "is nothing but" Smith, *Description of New England*, p. 14.

9   "Sometimes as many" from *Hinckley Township: Grand Lake Stream Plantation, A Sketch by Minnie Atkinson* (ca. 1920), in Turkel, "Canoeing the Eastern Maine Canoe Trail."

10 "Their Boats" Pring, "A Voyage...for the discouerie of the North part of Virginia...," in Quinn and Quinn, *English New England Voyages*, pp. 222–23.

11 "they in their Canoa" Rosier, *A True Relation*, in Quinn and Quinn, *English New England Voyages*, pp. 281–82.

11 "eel-weir place" Eckstorm, *Indian Place Names*, p. 15.

13 "to seeke out" in Morison, *European Discovery of America*, p. 159.

14 "It is to the southward" in Morison, *European Discovery of America*, p. 331.

15 "they affirm" in Hoffman, *Cabot to Cartier*, p. 11.

17–18 "While we thus sounded" Rosier, *Briefe and True Relation*, in Quinn and Quinn, *English New England Voyages*, pp. 286–87. The "whole company" numbered thirty-four men.

19 "eight Indians" Brereton, *Briefe and True Relation*, in Quinn and Quinn, *English New England Voyages*, p. 145.

20 "There are six months" in Lee, ed., *Maine: A Literary Chronicle*, p. 28.

21 "much bruised" Bradford, *Of Plymouth Plantation*, p. 64.

23 "furnish himself" in Quinn and Quinn, *English New England Voyages*, p. 460.

24 "no mynes discouered" "Davies Journal of the 1607 North Virginia Voyage," in Quinn and Quinn, *English New England Voyages*, p. 415.

25 Maine's First Ship, Inc., in Phippsburg, is planning to build a replica of *Virginia* before 2007.

27 "And of all" Smith, *Description of New England*, p. 6.

29 "fishing before your doors" Smith, *Description of New England*, pp. 10–11.

29 "It may also be" "A Treatise, conteining important inducements for the planting in these parts, and finding a passage that way to the South sea and China," in Quinn and Quinn, *English New England Voyages*, p. 176.

30 "for the better providing" in Malone, *Pine Trees and Politics*, p. 10.

32 "There is also" Samuel Pepys's Diary, Dec. 3, 1666, in Rowe, *Maritime History of Maine*, p. 33.

34	"to spend a lyttle time" in Faulkner and Faulkner, "Acadian Settlement," in Judd, et al., *Maine,* p. 87.
37	"Sawing plank" Chapelle, *History of American Sailing Ships,* p. 9.
38	"laid on the shores" in Morison, et al., *Concise History,* p. 32.
41	"their many sharp, steep Hills" Adams, *Diary and Autobiography,* vol. 1, p. 359.
41	"From Falmouth" Adams, *Diary and Autobiography,* vol. 3, p. 281.
42	"most of us" in Leamon, *Revolution Downeast,* p. 117.
42	"A horse" Sabine, "Moose Island" in Kilby, *Eastport and Passamaquoddy,* p. 158.
44–45	"My design" in Leamon, *Revolution Downeast,* p. 70.
46	"Could we then" in Leamon, *Revolution Downeast,* p. 239, no. 36.
49	"Resolved" in Paine, *Ships of the World,* p. 420.
50	"endeavour to divert" in Morison, et al., *Concise History,* p. 110.
51	"that their countrymen" in Alexander Hamilton, "Letters of Intruction," paragraph 14.
51–52	"the necessary support" in Gleason, *Kindly Lights,* p. 22.
52	"not a ship" William Willis, quoted in Dean, *Portland Marine Society,* p. 23.
53	"That leave might be given" in Morison, *Maritime History of Massachusetts,* p. 134.
54–55	"The nearer you approach" La Rochefoucault-Liancourt, in Candee, "The Appearance of Enterprise and Improvement" in Sprague, ed., *Agreeable Situations,* p. 67.
57	"more natural advantage" in Maloney, *Captain from Connecticut,* p. 211.
59	"A large number" in Butler, "Rising Like a Phoenix," in Sprague, *Agreeable Situations,* p. 27.
59	"no one ever heard" in Baker, *Maritime History of Bath,* p. 187.
59–60	"We accordingly" in Baker, *Maritime History of Bath,* p. 189.
69	Chapelle, *The Search for Speed under Sail.*
71	"very sharp" in Paine, *Ships of the World,* p. 480.
75	"Covering many a rood...." Longfellow, "The Building of the Ship," ll. 55–69. Longfellow does allow himself some poetic license, and his metaphorical reference to "ribs of steel" (l. 383) prefigures the actual use of steel in American shipbuilding by about three decades.
79	"the figure of" in Lubbock, *Down Easters,* p. 14.
80	"the advantage of position" Duncan, *Deepwater Family,* p. 154.
83	Cogill, *When God Was an Atheist Sailor,* p. 16.
85	Chapelle, *History of American Sailing Ships,* p. 219.

86   *Oxford English Dictionary.*

91   "like a star" Thoreau, *Maine Woods,* p. 655.

92   "They are light" Thoreau, *Maine Woods,* p. 595.

94   "constructed of" in Rivard, "Maine Manufactures, 1820–80," in Judd, et al., *Maine,* p. 331.

95   "old tubs" *Rockland Opinion,* Oct. 11, 1890, in Grindle, *Quarry and Kiln,* p. 89.

95   "most cold-blooded" *Rockland Opinion,* Mar. 2, 1900, in Grindle, *Quarry and Kiln,* p. 264.

98   "Eight Columns of Worship" is the title of an exhibit at the Vinalhaven Historical Society.

98–99   "granite was being taken" Hauk, *Stone Sloops of Chebeague,* p. 31.

103   "You have often expressed" in Druett, *She Captains,* p. 236.

105   "When you catch sight" Jewett, *Country By-Ways* (1881), in Winslow, *Piscataqua Gundalow,* p. 19.

106   "a booth" in Anderson, *Canals and Inland Waterways of Maine,* p. 150.

107   "float" in Anderson, *Canals and Inland Waterways of Maine,* p. 151.

107   "a well-known and eccentric citizen" Baker, *Maritime History of Bath,* p. 266.

109   "the keepers" United States, 25th Congress, 3d Session, *Executive Doc. No. 21,* pp. 21–23.

110   "Boston had no" Morison, *Maritime History of Massachusetts,* p. 236.

114   "dividends of 146 percent" Bowker, *Atlantic Four-Master,* p. 3.

114   "more than 900 wooden craft" see Duncan, *Coastal Maine,* pp. 490–91, and note p. 492.

115   Shipyard costs from Snow, *Bath Iron Works,* pp. 34–35.

115–16   "the most uncomfortable warship" in Allen, "USS *Katahdin.*"

120   "notwithstanding the efforts" George H. Procter, *The Fishermen's Memorial and Record Book* (Gloucester, MA: Procter Bros., 1873), in O'Leary, *Maine Sea Fisheries,* p. 222.

121   "the fish" United States, *Appendix to the Annals of Congress,* 2nd Congress, 1st Session (1792), Col. 1331, in O'Leary, *Maine Sea Fisheries,* p. 197.

131   "an established fact" in Conkling, *Islands in Time,* p. 236.

134–35   "You are riding" Stowe, "To the Editor," *National Era,* Aug. 5, 1852, in Shain and Shain, *Maine Reader,* p. 123.

135   "scenery so grand" J. L. Stevens, Jr., *Gloucester* [MA] *Daily Telegraph,* 11 Sept. 1850, in Wilmerding, *Paintings by Fitz Hugh Lane,* p. 120, 136.

136   "Here the sea" Norman, *Selected Writings of John Marin,* p. 171.

137   "even the prosaic" in Helfrich and O'Neil, *Lost Bar Harbor,* p. 5.

138   "a kind of fantastic" Vincent Scully, quoted in Helfrich and O'Neil, *Lost Bar Harbor,* p. 18.

138   "Oh, Lord" in Helfrich and O'Neil, *Lost Bar Harbor,* p. 9.

141   "The danger" in Rousmaniere, *Golden Pastime.*

144   "W. Starling Burgess" in Taylor, "Ranger," pp. 43–49.

149   "more than a good-sized" Snow, *Bath Iron Works,* p. 386.

155   "marine highway" Maine Department of Transportation, *Twenty-Year Transportation Plan,* p. 36.

156   "by opinion of others" Rosier, *True Relation,* in Quinn and Quinn, *English New England Voyages,* p. 290.

157   "the location" Powers, "Field of Dreams," *Mariner,* Fall 1999, p. 14.

157   "the way life should be" Unofficial motto of the State of Maine.

Bibliography

Adams, John. *Diary and Autobiography of John Adams.* Ed. L. H. Butterfield. 4 vols. Cambridge: Belknap Press, 1962.

Albion, Robert G. *The Rise of New York Port, 1815–1860.* 1939. Reprint Boston: Northeastern University Press, 1984.

Albion, Robert G., William A. Baker, and Benjamin W. Larabee. *New England and the Sea.* Revised edition. Mystic, CT: Mystic Seaport Museum, 1994.

Allen, Francis J. "USS *Katahdin*: Fighting Ram." *Warship* 47 (1988): 10–19.

Allin, Lawrence Carroll. "The Lime Coast: A Maritime Nexus of Community." In Timothy J. Runyan, ed., *Ships, Seafaring and Society: Essays in Maritime History.* Detroit, MI: Wayne State University Press, 1987.

Anderson, Hayden L. V. *Canals and Inland Waterways of Maine.* Maine Historical Society Research Series No. 2. Portland, ME: Maine Historical Society, 1982.

Bachelder, Peter Dow, and Mason Philip Smith. *Four Short Blasts: The Gale of 1898 and the Loss of the Steamer "Portland."* Portland, ME: Provincial Press, 1998.

Baker, William Avery. *A Maritime History of Bath and the Kennebec River Region.* 2 vols. Bath: Marine Research Society of Bath, 1973.

Banks, Ronald F. *A History of Maine: A Collection of Readings on the History of Maine 1600–1970.* Dubuque, IA: Kendall Hunt Publishing Co., 1969.

Barry, William David, and Francis W. Peabody. *Tate House: Crown of the Maine Mast Trade.* Portland: National Society of Colonial Dames of America in the State of Maine, 1982.

Bowker, Francis E. *Atlantic Four-Master: The Story of the Schooner "Herbert L. Rawding."* Mystic, CT: Mystic Seaport Museum, 1986.

Bradford, William. *Of Plymouth Plantation 1620–47.* Ed. Samuel Eliot Morison. New York: Alfred A. Knopf, 1954.

Brown, C. Donald. "Eastport: A Maritime History." *American Neptune* 28 (Apr. 1968): 113–27.

Butler, Joyce. "Rising Like a Phoenix: Commerce in Southern Maine, 1775–1830." In Laura Fecych Sprague, ed., *Agreeable Situations: Society, Commerce, and Art in Southern Maine, 1730–1830.* Kennebunk, ME: The Brick Store Museum, 1987.

Candee, Richard M. "'The Appearance of Enterprise and Improvement': Architecture and the Coastal Elite of Southern Maine," in Laura Fecych Sprague, ed., *Agreeable Situations: Society, Commerce, and Art in Southern Maine, 1730–1830.* Kennebunk, ME: The Brick Store Museum, 1987.

Chapelle, Howard I. *American Small Sailing Craft, Their Design, Development, and Construction*. New York: W. W. Norton, 1951.

——. *The History of American Sailing Ships*. New York: W. W. Norton, 1935.

——. *The Search for Speed under Sail, 1700–1855*. New York: W. W. Norton, 1967.

Cogill, Burgess. *When God Was an Atheist Sailor: Memories of a Childhood 1902–1910*. New York: W. W. Norton, 1990.

Conkling, Philip W. *Islands in Time: A Natural and Cultural History of the Islands of the Gulf of Maine*. 2nd ed. Rockland, ME: Island Institute/Camden, ME: Down East Books, 1999.

——, ed. *From Cape Cod to the Bay of Fundy: An Environmental Atlas of the Gulf of Maine*. Cambridge, MA: MIT Press, 1995.

Dean, Nicholas and John K. Moulton. *History of the Marine Society, 1796–1996: A Bicentennial History*. Portland, ME: Portland Marine Society, 1996.

Dean, Nick. "Recycling a Maine Island." *Down East* 29:1 (Aug. 1982): 112–17.

Druett, Joan. *She Captains: Heroines and Hellions of the Sea*. New York: Simon and Schuster, 2000.

Duncan, Fred B. *Deepwater Family*. New York: Pantheon Books, 1969.

Duncan, Roger. *Coastal Maine: A Maritime History*. New York: W. W. Norton, 1992.

Eckstorm, Fannie Hardy. *Indian Place Names of the Penobscot Valley and the Maine Coast*. Orono, ME: University of Maine Press, 1941.

Everson, Jennie G. *Tidewater Ice of the Kennebec River*. Maine Heritage Series No. 1. Augusta, ME: Maine State Museum, 1970.

Gleason, Sarah C. *Kindly Lights: A History of the Lighthouse of Southern New England*. Boston: Beacon Press, 1991.

Grindle, Roger L. *Quarry and Kiln: The Story of Maine's Lime Industry*. Rockland, ME: *Courier-Gazette*, 1971.

——. *Tombstones and Paving Blocks: The History of the Maine Granite Industry*. Rockland, ME: *Courier-Gazette*, 1977.

Haley, Neale. *The Schooner Era: A Lost Epic in History*. New York: A. S. Barnes & Co., 1972.

Hamilton, Alexander. "Letters of Instruction to the Commanding Officers of the Revenue Cutters." June 4, 1791. http:// www.uscg.mil/ HQ/G-CP/history/faqs/hamiltonletter.html

Hauk, Z. William, comp. *The Stone Sloops of Chebeague and the Men Who Sailed Them*. Boston & Chebeague: privately printed, 1949.

Helfrich, G. W. and Gladys O'Neil. *Lost Bar Harbor*. Camden, ME: Down East Books, 1982.

Hoffman, Bernard G. *Cabot to Cartier: Sources for a Historical Ethnography of Northeastern North America, 1497–1550*. Toronto: University of Toronto Press, 1961.

Holland, F. Ross, Jr. *Great American Lighthouses.* Washington, DC: Preservation Press, 1989.

Hutchins, John G. B. *The American Maritime Industries and Public Policy, 1789–1914: An Economic History.* New York: Russell and Russell, 1941.

Judd, Richard W., Edwin A. Churchill, and Joel W. Eastman. *Maine: The Pine Tree State from Prehistory to the Present.* Orono, ME: University of Maine Press, 1995.

Larabee, Benjamin W., ed. *The Atlantic World of Robert G. Albion.* Middletown, CT: Wesleyan University Press, 1975.

Leamon, James S. *Revolution Down East: The War for Independence in Maine.* Amherst, MA: University of Massachusetts Press, 1993.

Leavitt, John F. *Wake of the Coasters.* Middletown, CT: Wesleyan University Press, 1970.

Lee, W. Storrs, ed. *Maine: A Literary Chronicle.* New York: Funk & Wagnalls, 1968.

Longfellow, Henry Wadsworth. "The Building of the Ship." In volume 1 of *The Poetical Works of Henry Wadsworth Longfellow, with Bibliographical and Critical Notes.* Riverside Edition. Boston: Houghton, Mifflin, 1890.

Lubbock, Basil. *The Down Easters.* Glasgow: Brown Son & Ferguson, 1929.

Lyon, David John. *The Sailing Navy List.* London: Conway Maritime Press, 1993.

MacGregor, David R. *Merchant Sailing Ships 1850–1875.* London: Conway Maritime Press, 1984.

Maine Department of Transportation. *Twenty-Year Transportation Plan, 1998–2018.* Augusta, ME: Maine Department of Transportation, 1998.

Malone, Joseph J. *Pine Trees and Politics: The Naval Stores and Forest Policy in Colonial New England, 1691–1775.* Seattle, WA: University of Washington Press, 1964.

Maloney, Linda M. *The Captain from Connecticut: The Life and Times of Isaac Hull.* Boston: Northeastern University Press, 1986.

Martin, Kenneth R., *Whalemen and Whaleships of Maine.* Brunswick, ME: Harpswell Press, 1975.

Martin, Kenneth R. and Nathan R. Lipfert. *Lobstering and the Maine Coast.* Bath, ME: Maine Maritime Museum, 1985.

Morison, Samuel Eliot. *The European Discovery of America: The Northern Voyages.* New York: Oxford University Press, 1971.

——. *The Maritime History of Massachusetts 1783–1860.* Boston: Houghton Mifflin, 1941.

Morison, Samuel Eliot, Henry Steele Commager, and William E. Leuchtenburg. *A Concise History of the American Republic.* New York: Oxford University Press, 1979.

Morris, E. P. *The Fore-and-Aft Rig in America: A Sketch.* New Haven, CT: Yale University Press, 1927.

Morris, Paul C. *American Sailing Coasters of the North Atlantic.* New York: Bonanza, 1973.

——. *Four-Masted Schooners of the East Coast.* Orleans, MA: Lower Cape Publishing, 1975.

——. *Schooners and Schooner Barges.* Orleans, MA: Lower Cape Publishing, 1984.

Noble, Dennis L. *Lighthouses & Keepers: The U.S. Lighthouse Service and Its Legacy.* Annapolis, MD: Naval Institute Press, 1997.

Norman, Dorothy, ed. *Selected Writings of John Marin.* New York: Pellegrini and Cudahy, 1949.

O'Leary, Wayne M. *Maine Sea Fisheries: The Rise and Fall of a Native Industry, 1830–1890.* Boston: Northeastern University Press, 1996.

Paine, Lincoln P. *Ships of the World: An Historical Encyclopedia.* Boston: Houghton Mifflin, 1997.

Pike, Robert E. *Tall Trees, Tough Men.* New York: W. W. Norton, 1967.

Powers, Henry M. "The Field of Dreams: 'Build It and They Will Come.' The Fallacy of Port Development." *Mariner* (Fall 1999): 14–15.

Quinn, David B. and Alison M. Quinn, eds. *The English New England Voyages 1602–1608.* London: Hakluyt Society, 1983.

Ridgely-Nevitt, Cedric. *American Steamships on the Atlantic.* New York: University of Delaware Press, 1981.

Rindlaub, Curtis. *The Maine Coast Guide for Small Boats: Casco Bay.* Peak's Island, ME: Diamond Pass Publishing, 2000.

Robinson, William F. *Coastal New England.* Boston: New York Graphic Society, 1983.

Rousmaniere, John. *The Golden Pastime: A New History of Yachting.* New York: W. W. Norton, 1986.

Rowe, William Hutchinson. *A Maritime History of Maine: Three Centuries of Shipbuilding and Seafaring.* New York: W. W. Norton, 1948.

——. *Shipbuilding Days in Casco Bay, 1727–1890: Being Footnotes to the Maritime History of Maine.* Freeport, ME: Bond Wheelwright Co., 1929.

Sabine, Lorenzo. "Moose Island." In William Henry Kilby, ed., *Eastport and Passamaquoddy.* Eastport, ME: Edward E. Shead & Co., 1888.

Sawtelle, Joseph G., ed. *John Paul Jones and the "Ranger": Portsmouth, New Hampshire, July 12–November 1, 1777, and the Log of the "Ranger" November 1, 1777–May 18, 1777.* Portsmouth, NH: Portsmouth Marine Society, 1994.

Shain, Charles and Samuella Shain, eds. *The Maine Reader: The Down East Experience from 1614 to the Present.* Boston: David R. Godine, 1991.

Smith, Horatio Davis. *Early History of the United States Revenue Marine*

Service (or United States Revenue Cutter Service) 1789–1849. Washington, DC: Naval Historical Foundation, 1932.

Smith, John. *A Description of New England....*1616. Reprint, Washington, DC: P. Force, 1837.

Smith, Mason Philip. *Confederates Downeast: Confederate Operations in and Around Maine.* Portland, ME: Provincial Press, 1985.

Snow, Ralph Linwood. *Bath Iron Works: The First Hundred Years.* Bath, ME: Maine Maritime Museum, 1987.

Snow, Ralph Linwood, and Douglas K. Lee. *A Shipyard in Maine: Percy & Small and the Great Schooners.* Gardiner, ME: Tilbury House, Publishers/Maine Maritime Museum, 1999.

Sprague, Laura Fecych, ed., *Agreeable Situations: Society, Commerce, and Art in Southern Maine, 1730–1830.* Kennebunk, ME: The Brick Store Museum, 1987.

Taft, Hank, Jan Taft, and Curtis Rindlaub. *A Cruising Guide to the Maine Coast.* 2nd ed. Peaks Island, ME: Diamond Pass Publishing, 1996.

Taylor, William H. "*Ranger*, The American Defender." *Yachting* 62 (Aug. 1937): 43–49.

Thoreau, Henry David. *The Maine Woods.* In *A Week on the Concord and Merrimack Rivers. Walden; or Life in the Woods. The Maine Woods. Cape Cod.* New York: Library of America, 1985.

Thorndike, Virginia L. *Maine Lobsterboats: Builders and Lobstermen Speak of Their Craft.* Camden, ME: Down East Books, 1998.

Tod, Giles M. P. *The Last Sail Down East.* Barre, MA: Barre Publishing, 1965.

Turkel, Tux. "Canoeing the Eastern Maine Canoe Trail." *Portland Press Herald,* "Vacationland Guide," Sunday, July 28, 1996, p. 39.

United States, 25th Congress, 3d Session, *Executive Doc. No. 21* (13 Dec., 1838), pp. 21–23. Letter from Jos. T. Sherwood to Hon. John Anderson, Collector of Customs.

Upton, Joe. *Amaretto.* Camden, ME: International Marine Publishing Co., 1986.

Webb, Robert Lloyd, curator. *Edward O'Brien: Shipbuilder of Thomaston: An Exhibition, 25 May 1990 to 19 May 1991.* Bath, ME: Maine Maritime Museum, 1990.

Wilmerding, John. *Paintings by Fitz Hugh Lane.* Washington, DC: National Gallery of Art, 1988.

Wilson, Jon. "Voyage of the Improbable: Recollections of *WoodenBoat.*" *WoodenBoat* 150 (Sept./Oct. 1999): 32–36.

Winslow, Richard E., III. *The Piscataqua Gundalow: Workhorse for a Tidal Basin Empire.* Portsmouth, NH: Portsmouth Marine Society, 1983.

Wood, Richard G. *A History of Lumbering in Maine 1820–1861.* University of Maine Studies, Second Series, No. 33. Orono, 1935.

Index

LINCOLN PAXTON PAINE is a maritime historian, author, and teacher. As co-chair of OpSail Maine 2000's education committee, he was one of the principal architects of the Maine Maritime Heritage Trail. His highly acclaimed *Ships of the World: An Historical Encyclopedia* (Houghton Mifflin, 1997) was among the books named "Best of Reference 1998" by the New York Public Library. He lives in Portland with his wife and two daughters.